A Glossary of the Dorset Dialect, with a Grammar of Its Wording

William Barnes

Nabu Public Domain Reprints:

You are holding a reproduction of an original work published before 1923 that is in the public domain in the United States of America, and possibly other countries. You may freely copy and distribute this work as no entity (individual or corporate) has a copyright on the body of the work. This book may contain prior copyright references, and library stamps (as most of these works were scanned from library copies). These have been scanned and retained as part of the historical artifact.

This book may have occasional imperfections such as missing or blurred pages, poor pictures, errant marks, etc. that were either part of the original artifact, or were introduced by the scanning process. We believe this work is culturally important, and despite the imperfections, have elected to bring it back into print as part of our continuing commitment to the preservation of printed works worldwide. We appreciate your understanding of the imperfections in the preservation process, and hope you enjoy this valuable book.

JUST PUBLISHED. Price 6s. Demy 8vo.
(*Uniform in size with the* ENGLISH DIALECT SOCIETY'S
PUBLICATIONS, *and will bind with them.*)

A GRAMMAR & GLOSSARY
OF THE
DORSET DIALECT.

BY

THE REV. WILLIAM BARNES,
(*Late Rector of Winterborne Came*).

AUTHOR OF "POEMS IN THE DORSET DIALECT,"
"ANGLO-SAXON GRAMMAR," &c., &c.

"This is decidedly one of the best Dialect Glossaries we have ever seen. Mr. Barnes' charming "Poems of Rural Life" has given to the Dorset Dialect a literary interest which is possessed by no other of the local varieties of English rustic speech."
Athenæum

"The Dorset poet has performed his task with his accustomed skill and thorough acquaintance with the Folk-Speech of his native shire."—*Dorset County Chronicle.*

"Not only a curiosity of literature, but a valuable addition to our knowledge."—*Saturday Review.*

"Stamped with the seal of genuine originality, and gleaming from page to page in unaffected local colour."—*Spectator.*

"The Dorsetshire Dialect has some philological interest and much originality, has been raised to literary rank by the learned rector of Winterborne Came."—*Illustrated London News.*

DORCHESTER:
M. & E. CASE, BOOKSELLERS, CORNHILL.
LONDON:
TRÜBNER & Co, LUDGATE HILL.
And all Booksellers.

J. Haldon & Son
95 Long Street
Bedford Road
Manchester

A GLOSSARY
OF THE
DORSET DIALECT
WITH A
GRAMMAR
OF ITS
WORD SHAPENING AND WORDING.

BY
WILLIAM BARNES, B.D.
AUTHOR OF "POEMS OF RURAL LIFE," IN THE DORSET DIALECT.

DORCHESTER:
M & E. CASE, COUNTY PRINTERS, 4, CORNHILL.
LONDON:
TRÜBNER & Co., LUDGATE HILL.
1886.
[*ALL RIGHTS RESERVED.*]

FORE NOTES.

DORSET.

THE Dorset form of folk-speech, like other English ones, is one of words differing more or less from those of book English in sundry ways.

I.

(1) Of words of the same meaning and nearly of the same shape as those of book-English ones, from which they differ only in voicings, or breathpennings. In voicings, as

   Bwone, bone.
   Ceäke, cake.
   Doust, dust.
   Meäd, mead.

(2) In breathpennings

   Coose, course.
   Drong, throng.
   Hapse, hasp.
   Zing, sing.

II.

In words of the same shapes as book-English ones, or differing from them only slighly, as in voicing or breathpenning, but having a broader or narrower meaning than the common ones, such as with a broader meaning

   Praïse.
   Steäre. }
   Stare. }
   Starve, to stiffen.

III.

Dorset shapes of old English words now quite or almost out of use, as

   Anon, immediately.
   Avore, afore.

Culver.
Cwoffer.
Dapper.
Fall.
Handsel.
Heal.
Knap.
Leer.
Lwoth.
Nêsh.
Rathe.

IV.

Words from the same roots as matching English, but of other forms of stemwords

Pank, pant.
Bunt, butt.
Cleadon, cleavers.
Dunch, deafish.
Dunchnettle, deadnettle.
Spreathe, spray.

V.

Words from English roots or stems, for which common English has some words from other roots or stems.

Bleäre, low.
Eltrot, } cow parsely.
Eltroot }
Ho's-tinger, dragon fly.
Clote, yellow water lily.
Peze, ooze.
Reem, stretch.
Silgreen, houseleek.
Nêsh, tender.

VI.

Words for which common English has not any of the same meaning, such as

Drashel.
Hile.
Hick.
Lewth.
Moot.
Pont.
Snag.
Squinch.

VII.

Words beyond those which Dorset has in common with English, from the same roots, but words shapen lawfully by the use of the particles, as headings or endings.

The ending i c has a lessening meaning, as

Hood, Hudddick, D. A small hood for a sore finger.

    Par, parrick, D.
    Red, ruddick.
    Whine, whinnick, D.
    Dun, dunnick.
    Rangle.
    Ringle.
    Shockle.
    Ruggle.
    Pope, puppet.
    Knog, nugget.

VIII.

Words for which book English has, or uses only foreign ones.

    Fay, succeed.
    Gregle, hyacinth.
    Goolden chaïn, laburnum.
    Headlong, precipitate.
    Meädon, camomile.

In 1844 a Glossary of the Dorset was printed and published with the first edition of the first collection of the Dorset poems. In 1847 a 2nd edition of the first collection was published by J. R. Smith, without a Glossary, 18 sheets, demy 12 mo. 1863 the Philological Society printed for their transactions, a corrected and fuller Glossary of the Dorset Dialect, with the history, outspreading, and bearing of the South Western English, 8 vo, p. p. 103. Published for the Philological Society by Asher & Co., Berlin.

Since then the Editor of the *Dorset County Chronicle* kindly put into his paper weekly shares of that Glossary, headed by the following request—"The Dorset Dialect.—It is wished for the 'English Dialect Society,' and for the sake of the history of the English language, to collect any Dorset (provincial) words which are not found in Mr. Barnes' Glossary, and we hope to print, from time to time, the words of the Glossary, in portions, with a hope that some of our Dorset readers will kindly write off any other word that may be heard in their neighbourhoods, or and other meanings of those which we may give, and send them to the Rev. W. Barnes, Came Rectory, Dorchester." Upon which several readers kindly sent me in from the corners of the shire, many more words which had lurked from my knowledge, so that I believe I have now the field of Dorset folk speech as clean as I can well hope to leave it.

I do not wish it to be understood that my so called Glossary of the Dorset Dialect contains no Dorset words which are used outside of Dorset.

A correspondent of a Dorset paper, lately gave the opinion that it was quite wrong that I had given as Dorset words many that were not peculiar to the county. Let us try this canon in wort lore, let it be granted that a rather rare species of heath plant should be found near Poole, and again at Bournemouth in Hampshire. Then, no writer on the Flora of Dorset, should put it into his list, since it is found in Hampshire, and so no writer on the Flora of Hants, should put it into his list, because it is found in Dorset; and no list of plants of any other shire should have it, because it is found in those two—and so it must not be put into the Flora of England. And so with Dorset words, none that are used out of Dorset are to be put into the word list of any County of England—*a reductio ad absurdum.*

The forms of folk speech do not change at the map boundaries of Counties, but rather at ridges of hills and streams, as at the river Parret, where there is a sudden change from the old Wessex to the Devon shape, and there are words and word forms in the Vale of Blackmore, which have not come over the chalk downs, on the south of the Vale, but, there is no perceptible change of speech within the three miles between Gillingham, Dorset, and Mere, Wilts.

We want to find how wide spread is the use of a word and how and whence it came on to its grounds, for it may be Saxon, or Welsh, or Norman, or may have been brought from Friesland; as the word BIBBER in the Glossary.

In somewhat of a merry mood, I was one day minded to see how far our homely Dorset speech could give the meaning of the seemingly ministerial wording of the so-called Queen's speech on the opening of Parliament in 1884. Her Majesty's speech as written and read in Her Majesty's name. Here are samples of a few clauses—

"My Lords and Gentlemen,—The satisfaction with which I ordinarily release you from discharging the duties of the Session is on the present occasion qualified by a sincere regret that an important part of your labours should have failed to result in a legislative enactment."

(1) The lightheartedness I do mwostly veel when I do let ye off vrom the business upon your hands in the Sessions, is theäse time a little bit damped, owen to a ranklen in my mind, that a goodish lot o' your work vell short o' comen into anything lik laws.

"The most friendly intercourse continues to subsist between myself and all foreign Powers.'

(2) The very best o' veelens be still a-kept up, in deälens between myzelf an' all o' the outlandish powers.

"Diplomatic relations have been resumed with Mexico, and a preliminary agreement has been signed, providing for the negotiation of a new Treaty of Commerce and Navigation."

(3) Zome deälèns have a-been a-took up ageän wi' Mexico, an' we've bwoth a-put our hands to an understanden-like that we'd meäke a new bargain about treäde and seafeärèn.

"I have to lament the failure of the efforts which were made by the European Powers assembled in the recent Conference to devise means for restoring that equilibrium in the finances of Egypt which is so important an element in its well-being and good order."

(4) I can't but be ever so zorry that nothèn come out o' the doèns o' the Girt Powers o' Europe that put their heads together tother day in. the girt talking a' tryèn to vind out zome way o' puttèn to rights ageân the money-stock ov Egypt, a thing that do goo so vur towards the well-beèn and well-dooèn o't.

"My Lords and Gentlemen,—I continue to view with unabated satisfaction the mitigation and diminution of agrarian crime in Ireland, and the substantial improvement in the condition of its people."

(5) I do still zee to my unlessened happiness how vield crimes be a milden'd and a lessen'd in Ireland, and in what a soundly bettered plight be the vo'k.

In the following words, whether Dorset or common English, the one sounded *ea* would be pronounced as the sound 2 in the table, page 1, though in English they have the sound 1 in the table.

> Beach, bleach, breach
> Cease, creak
> Deal
> Eat
> Glean
> Heal
> Meal, meat
> Neat
> Pea, peaze, peat
> Read, ream
> Seam, seat
> Teal, teaze
> Veal
> Wean, wheat

Of this sound, is *e* in some one-sounded words, as mesh, nesh, plesh.

The two-sounded *eä* are marked in the small type of the Grammar and in the Poems. (*See* pages 2 and 3 of the Grammar.)

OUTLINE OF THE GRAMMAR OF THE DORSET DIALECT.

VOICE SOUNDS.

1 ee in meet.
2 ee the Dorset ê.
3 a in mate.
4 ea in earth, or the French e in le.
5 a in father.
6 aw in awe.
7 o as in rope.
8 oo as in food.

These 8 sounds are found in Dorset, both short and long, whereas the 2nd, the Dorset ê, is unheard, as a long one, in book-English. It is a second between that of *ee* in meet, and *a* in mate; and, although it is often, if not mostly, heard in English as that of *i* in bid, (which is neither *beed*, nor *bed*,) yet it is not easily voiced as a long sound by others than Dorset or western people. It is I believe owned as a long sound by the Magyar speech.

The tendency (known in Latin,) of an open vowel in the root to become a close one, in the clustered word, or in a low-strained breathsound, holds in the English, and more in Dorset. As in Latin, *salio*, yields *insilio*, so from the stems

Man we have huntsman: pronounced huntsmin, i = 4,
Spell   ,,   Gospel: ,,   Gospil,   i = 4,
Ford   ,,   Blandford: ,,   Blandfird,   i = 4,
House   ,,   Malthouse: ,,   Malthis,   i = 4,
Coat   ,,   Waistcoat: ,,   Waistcit,   i = 4,
Bord }   Board } ,,   Starboard: ,,   Starbird,   i = 4.

I.—The sound 1 long *ee* is in some Dorset words the like sound as

    bee, free, he, need, peep, reap, weed,

Though sometimes a little shorter than in English.

I.—The sound 1 of *ea*, in some other English words is in Dorset a twysound 1.4 as

    bean, clean, lean, mead.
   D. beän, cleän, leän, meäd.

I.—In other words again the English sound 1 of *ea* becomes, in Dorset, a single sound 2 of the Dorset, ê 2, as

    bead, meat, read.
   D. bêd, mêt, rêd.

These three sundry shapes for the English sound 1 are not without some grounds of difference in the Saxon shapes of the words

   leap, *Saxon*, hleap, *Dorset*, leäp.
   meat, *Saxon*, mète, *Dorset*, mêt.

So from the Saxon twysound the Dorset has a twysound, and from the Saxon single sound it has a single one, the English spelling notwithstanding.

This sound 1 has a tendency in Ireland, and in Norfolk, and therefore in the eastern counties, to become *a* = 3, as in "a hape, or a dale o' whate," a heap, or a deal of wheat, in Norfolk, and "a grate dale o' work" in Ireland.

The Norfolk men are Angles, and therefore, as truly English, they should speak better English than is that of us of the under tribe of Saxons in the west . and who knows but that *dale* and *whate* are the sounds of the old *dæl*, and *hwaete* of the early English.

1·4·7.

The sound 1 short, given by 1 in some English words often becomes in Dorset 4 or even 7, as

    bridge, ridge, will,
   D. brudge, rudge, woll, wull.

In the Vale of Blackmore *will*, is at different times, *will*, *wull*, and *wooll*, even in the same mouth; and Mr. Halbertsma, a Friesian, says, in a work on the Friesic and Anglo-Saxon, "in the village where I was born, we said, indiscriminately, *after*, *efter*, and *æfter*."

So *wolle* and *woll*, for *will*, is found in the "Harrowing of Hell," a mirical-play of the time of Edward II. :—

'With resoun wolle ich haven hym :' 'With reason will I have them.'
'Reasoun wol y telle the :' 'I will tell thee a reason.'

So dame Juliana Barnes in her book on "Fysshynge" writes "I woll."

The long *e* 2 in Dorset speech is a sound between that of *ee* 1 in meet and *a* 3 in mate.

3. to 2.

The sound 3 short becomes in some Dorset words the Dorset 2 as

      day, edge, head, hedge, lead (plumbum), men, net, red, whey,
D. dê, idge, hid, hidge, lid,   min, nit, rid, whê.

3. to 1. 3.

For 3 long in *a* the Dorset has mostly 1 and 3.

      bake, cake, late, made, trade,
   D. beäke, ceäke, leäte, meäde, treäde.

As the Spanish has

      bien, cierto, invierno, sierra, tiempo, viento,

for the Italian

      bene, certo, inverno, serra, tempo, vento,

so

"What have you made of the old lame mare that you were leading up the lane from the mead"

would be in Dorset

"What have ye a-meäde o' the wold leäme meäre that you wer a-leadèn up leäne vrom the meäd."

The change of the English sound = 3 into some such diphthong as 1. 3. is holden in the north as well as the west. I have marked it in ten of the northern English versions of Bible books, printed by H. H. Prince Lucien Bonaparte, though, in Mr. Robson's metrical Song of Solomon. I find 3. 1 or 4. 1 for 3, as *teyste*, taste, *pleyce*, place.

3. to 5.

For 3 (short *e*) Dorset often takes 5 *a*,

    beg, egg, keg, leg, peg,
   D. bag, agg, kag, lag, pag.

AY.—3.1. to 5.1.

The English breathsounds *ay* 3.1. are in Dorset 5.1.

    Baÿ, gaÿ, haÿ, maÿ, paÿ, staÿ.

1.4. or 1.5.

In a few words the sound 4. of *ea* becomes in Dorset a twy-sound 1.3. or 1.4.

    earn, learn, fern,
    eärn, 1.5, leärn, veärn.

5. to 3.

In Blackmore *a* 5 become 3 as

    father, half, calf,
    faether, haef, caef.

In a few words (5 to 1.5. or 1.4) as in *ar*

    arm, D. eärm 1.5
    garden, D. geärden 1.4.

6.1. to 8.4.1.—*Oi* to *wei*.

    boil, point, spoil, coin.
   D. bweile, pweint, spweil, cwein.

    Joy however is jaÿ, 5.1.

oi in Norfolk become 4.1. as

    vice, spile, for voice, spoil.

6. to 3.

    law, daw, straw,
   D. lae, dae, strae.

    (*Blackmore*.)
    strawberry, straeberry.

6. to 5.

    born, corn, horn, storm.

A little flatter than (6) almost

    barn, carn, harn, starm.

7 into 8.4

    bold, cold, told, mold, oak,
   D. bwold, cwold, twold, mwold, woak.

7 to 4.8.   crust, dust, rut,
              D. croust, doust, rout.

In Northumberland and Scotland

7 is 6
              blow, show,
              blaw, shaw.

7 into 8
              go, so, toe,
           D. goo, zoo, too.

So in Norfolk
              spoke, spook.

Loo and *go* are put as fellow rhime-words in a copy of verses on Robert Nevile's "Poor Scholars," in Langbaine's "Dramatick Poets," 1691.

    "We'll change the song and cry as truly *too*,
      Whither may not this thy poor scholar *go*."

Whether it was *to* for *too*, or *goo* for *go*, is not clear.

The English tongue is much given to make the long O.4 a twysound, as it is in the folk-speech of the North, as well as that of Wessex.

I have found it in six of the Bible versions of H. H. Prince Lucien Buonaparte, under the forms 2.5, 6.1, 7.5, 8.5, 8.6.

In many cases our long O.7 takes the form of 1.2, 1.3 or 7.4 in Friesic, and I think that there is with Londoners a readiness to call a stone a stown (7.8).

A leaning to two sounds is found in most of the Teutonic tongues, and those of Dorset are upholden by those of Saxon and Friesic speech,

as beäm,	beam.	heört,	heart.
beö,	be.	meärc,	mark.
ceälf,	calf.	neöd,	need.
deäth,	death.	preöst,	priest.
eäld,	old.	reäm,	membrame.
feormer,	farmer.	seöfon,	seven.
geät,	gate.	weöd,	weed.

"And we sceölon meärcian ure foreweard heäfod,"
And we shall mark our forehead (forward head).

In West Friesian

beäm,	beam tree.	heäp,	heap.
doär,	door.	leäd, liëd,	lead.
deäd,	dead.	neät,	naught.
eästen,	east.	neäme,	to name.
foär,	fore.	seä,	sea.
goäld,	gold.	sliëp,	sleep.
heärde,	heard.	stiën,	stone.

In West Friesian even many of our short vowels are diphthongs,

breä',	bread.	oäf,	of.
fuöt,	foot.	roäst,	rust.
fuör,	for.	soän,	son.
oän,	on.	thoärst,	thirst.

and

Deär iz en griëne leäf uwt-shetten,
There is a green leaf out-shot.
Hiër rint en schiëp, deär giët en kuw,
Here run'th a sheep, there goeth a cow.

8.17

So in West Friesian,

Trog tjöck en tin,
Through thick and thin.

It is markworthy that *th* (10) has given way to *d* (9) in Sussex, as in

dis, dat, dem, dere,
for this, that, them, there.

BREATH PENNINGS.

The sounds of speech are given by sundry breathings under sundry pennings of the breath through the mouth.

There are two kinds of breath pennings.

The sounds AK, AP, AT, AG, AD, end with a dead penning of the breath, betokened by K, P, T, G, D. In AK and AG, it is pent in the throat. In AP and AB with the lips. In AT and AD, on the roof.

K.P.T. are hard pennings, G.B.D. are mild pennings—the breathing being harder in the former than in the latter three; then there are half-pennings of the sounding breath, which is more or less, though not wholly pent, but allowed to flow on through the nose as

        AMH, AM,
        ANH, AN.
        ANG.

or as in the sounds

AKH,	
AF,	AV,
ATH,	ATHE,
ALL, (Welsh),	AL,
ARH,	AR,
AS,	AZ,
ASH,	AJ.

half pent by the tongue and roof.

1 Dead Pennings, Hard.	2 Half Pennings, Hard.	3 Dead Pennings, Mild.	4 Half Pennings, Mild.
(1) CK,	(5) KH, (Germ. Welsh, Per.)	(14) G,	(18) GH.
(2) NK,	(6) F.	(15) NGH, NG,*	(19) NG.
(3) P,	(7) MH.	(16) B,	(20) V, BH (Irish)
(4) T,	(8) TH (in thick)	(17) D,	(21) M.
	(9) LL, (Welsh)		(22) TH (in thee)
	(10) RH, (Welsh)		(23) L.
	(11) S.		(24) R.
	(12) SH.		(25) Z.
	(13) NH.		(26) J. (French)
			(27) N.

*In finger not singer.

NK.

The Dorset has kept the older *nk*, and not taken the later *nch* in

             wink,   winch.

In Dorset, as in other tongues, there are cases of over-wielding among breath-pennings, of cases in which a penning when it touches another of an unlike kind, so far overwields it as to mould it into a form like its own—for 'thank God' we often say 'thang God.' *K* in thank is a hard penning, and *G* in God is its soft form, and the *k* on touching of the *g* is in Dorset often moulded into *g*.

4 T.

T is often left out from among other unlike breath-pennings.

Bistnot, } Bistn't, }	Bis'nt'
Giltcup,	Gil'cup.
Just,	Jis.'

6   20
F   V.

In Dorset.

The English hard penning (2) F often becomes the mild penning V (4),

    Feed, fetch, fast, fall, fore, foot, find.
D. Veed, vetch, vast, vall, vore, voot, vind.

But the Dorset does not hold *V* for *F* in words that are brought in from other and not Teutonic languages. We must say *Factory, false, family, famine, figure,* in Dorset, as well as in English.

In Swedish *f* is pronounced as *v* at the end of a word; *Gif lif at den bild :* 'Give life to the image,' being pronounced '*Giv liv at den bild :*' and the *f* of High-Dutch is, by the same smoothing of the pronunciation, worn into *v* in Low-Dutch:

High-Dutch,	fett,	frau,	fier	freund.
Low-Dutch,	vett,	vrouw,	vier,	vriend.
English,	fat,	woman,	four,	friend.

"Vixen has survived to us in the true sense in rustic speech only.

OF THE DORSET AND SOUTH-WESTERN DIALECT.

Grim told Kemble he was much surprised at this *v* in vixen, from *fox*; and one would perhaps have as soon looked for *filly*, from *foal*."—*Mr. Vernon.*

"The voxe hird," for "the fox heard," is found in a song of the fourteenth century, in which we find also, 'In pes withoute vyhte,' for 'In peace without fight.'

```
   8           17
   Th          D.
```

Th (8) of the English sometimes, and mostly before *r*, becomes D (17), as *drow* for throw; *drough*, through; *drash*, thrash; *drong*, throng; *droat*, throat; *drashel*, threshold. So in German,

die,	tod,	haide,	denken,	du,	dank,
the,	death,	heath,	think,	thou	thank,
dann,	diese,	dick,	ding,	dorn,	donner,
then,	these,	thick,	thing,	thorn,	thunder.

Th (8) is the smooth *th* (22) in some Dorset words, as

thaw, thimble, thin,
think, thistl, (thistle).

The hard breathing *h* is retained in some words from which book English has lost it, we say

Hwing for wing.
Hring for ring.

The H being the Saxon for an earlier K as in the Priesic
Kring.

10 for 24.—R.

R as a wordhead is, as it was often, if not always in Anglo-Saxon, hard breathed, as

rag,	hrag.
ram,	hram.
rand,	hrand.
rap,	hrap.
red,	hred.
reed,	hreed.
reef,	href.
reap,	hreap.
rib,	hrib.

rick,	hrick.
rim,	hrim.
rip,	hrip.
rob,	hrob.
rock,	hrock.
rod,	hrod.
row,	hrow.
rub,	hrub.
rue,	hrue.
rug,	hrug.
room,	hroom.

So Dorset is at one with the Anglo-Saxon in the breathing of

hraefen,	hraven.
hreac,	hrick.
hreod,	hreed.
hreol,	hreel.
hrime,	hrimè.
hring,	hring.
hróf,	hroof.

So Dorset has kept the hard breathed W, in some words from which it is often dropped, as

hwey,	whey.
hwarf,	wharf.
hwing,	wing.

He hrode by hroughest hroads, and hrugged hrocks where hrobbers hroamed.

24. 11.
R. S.

The Dorset is strongly given to drop *r* before *s*, as

scarce,	skease.
sarcenet,	sa·cenet.
scorse,	scuo·se.
worse,	wo·s.
orchard,	orcha·d.
fardle,	fa·dle.

birthday,	be·thday.
burst,	bu·rst.
course,	coo·se.
curse,	cu·ss.
dorser,	do·sser.
earth,	e·th.
forse,	fwo·se.
forth,	vwo·th.
hearth,	he·th.
hearse,	he·ss.
hoarse,	hwo·se.
horse,	ho·s.
mercy,	ma·cy.
nurse,	nu·s.
purse,	pu·s.

So in Latin the *r* seems to have been dropped in the cases of

Aes, mas, flos, os.
Aeris, maris, floris, oris.

Conversely, *th* (22) is put in Dorset for the English *d*: as blather, a bladder; lather, a ladder.

By Z for S Dutch differs from German.

11.   1.
 S.   K.

So with SK.

English, ask.
Dorset, ax.
Saxon, axiœan.

English, ashes.
Dorset, axan.
Saxon, axan.
Friesian, yesk.

Saxon. On haeran and on axan. (Matt. c. xi.)
Friesian. In sek and yeske.
Saxon. Betweox tham timple and tham weofode.
Friesian. Twisk di timple int it altar.

If it be asked who had the older form or who shifted the pennings, the truth seems to be that the Saxons seem to have shifted some of the clippings, as they surely shifted the *sk* or *sg* of the British word *Esk*, of which they made the *ex*, E*ks*.

11.   3.
S.   P.

There has been in the new or older forms of speech a stead-shifting of *s* with *p*.

    English.   Clasp, crisp, hasp. wasp.
    Dorset.   Claps, crips, haps, waps.
    Saxon.   Haeps, waeps.
    Holstein.   Waeps.

11.   3.
S.   P.

"Haps the geäte," said a mother to her boy behind her; "He'll haps hisself" was the answer.

11.4.11.—S.T.S.

For the shocking cluster of hard breathpennings *sts* in such words as chests, fists, posts, the Dorset wisely put a breathsound *e* after the *t*, and give istes, as chestes, vistes, postes, as ought to be done in Queen's English, in which the *ists* are enough to make an Italian or Maori shudder.

11.   25.
S.   L.

For hard *s* (15) English the Dorset holds, in many English words, the kinsletter *z*, as *s* in High-Dutch becomes *z* in Holland.

    E.   see, set, sand, sorry, sun.
    D.   zee, zet, zand, zorry, zun.

s-headed words however, which had come in, of later times, from other tongues keep the *s* sound in Dorset; as

         scene,   servant,   sabbath.
         scene,   sarvant,   sabbath.

Some pairs of like-sounded, *s*-headed, English words are distinguished in Dorset by *s* and *z*:

E.	D.	E.	D.
{ sea,	sea.	sun,	zun.
see,	zee.	son,	son.

{ set, (verb)	zet.	fowl,	vowl.
set, (noun)	set.	foul,	foul.

S as a word-head has a strengthening force, as

> creak,
> s.creak, to creak very strongly.
> crunch.
> s.crunch.

We want in England a prince, or an academy to give us a warrant for *es* instead of *s* only, and also for the good old ending *en* instead of the *hiss*, as coasten, ghosten.

D is sometimes dropped after *n* as in

> bran', brand.
> han', hand.
> poun', pound.
> roun', round.

There has been, either in the new, or older forms of speech, a metathesis not only of *s* with *p*, as

English,	clasp,	crisp,	hasp,	wasp,
Dorset,	claps,	crips,	haps,	waps,
Saxon-Eng.,	axian,	—	hæps,	waeps.

but of *s* with *k*.

Our Friesian bretheren have not the Saxon or Dorset order of the clippings.

Saxon-Eng.,	On haeran and on *axan*.
	Matt. c. xi.
Friesian,	Yn sek ind *yeske*.
Saxon-Eng.,	Betweox tham temple and them weofode.
Friesian,	*Twisk* di timple int it alter.
	Between the temple and the altar.

The truth seems to be that the metathesis began with the Saxon-English, as we know that the British word *esk*, Welsh *wysg*, a stream of water, became with them, *Ex* or *Ax*, as in *Exmouth*, *Ax-knoller*.

So the Saxon-English had

	cræt,	gaers,	forst,	flax,	fixas,
for	cart,	grass,	frost,	flask,	fishes.

and the Latin *marmor* is the Russian *mramor*.

20.   16.
V.   B.

When V and N (either in *en* as a wordending, or the pronoun *en*) come together, the *v* often overwields the *n* which in its new form overwields the *v* that becomes *b*.

N is a roof penning and a nose breathing, and *v* is a lip and teeth penning and a lip breathing. In the word EVEN the *v* may overwield *n* and bring it into a lip penning like itself by turning it into *m*, because *m* is a nose-breathing like *n*. Thus EVEN becomes

EVEM and *EVM*.

But M is a full-lip penning and so V shifts into a full dead lip-penning B and EVM becomes EBM. Thence the Dorset,

elebm,	eleven.
ebm,	even.
habm,	have-en, have him.
heabm,	Heaven.
obm,	oven.
sebm,	seven.

So with B or P before the pronoun EN,

drubm,	drub him.
mobm,	mob him.
robm,	rob him.
rubm,	rub him.
scrubm,	scrub him.
dropm,	drop him.
ztopm,	stop him.

The M as a mild penning, sometimes mildens the P into B, as

obn for open, opm.

In Latin P overwields N and makes it a lip-penning, as

in-pono,   impono.

In Persian, Gunbad becomes Gumbad.

23.	21.
L.	M.

L and M are in some words sundered by E,

        elm,   helm,   overwhelm.
        elem, helem, overwhelem.

24.11.

  r before *s* or *th* is so commonly dropped in Dorset as to afford a good sample of the working of Grimm's Law, that like cases take like changes.

24.	17.
R.	D.

R. 24.23.

  The liquids such as *rl* often take *d* or otherwise *e* between them ·

        twirl, twirdl, or twirel.
        harl, hardl, „ harrel.
        curl, curdl, „ currel.
        purl, purdl, „ purrel.

So the British *pen*, head, seems to have become, in Cornoak, *pedn*, and in Norfolk a *banner* is a *bander*, as they say all *mander* of colours.

27.	20.	6.
N.	B.	E.

The roof-penning N (27) before the lip-penning B (20) or F (6) may be overwielded by the B or F and shifted into M a lip-penning like itself, as

    1. bound bailiff, with *d* out.
       boun' bailie.
       bum bailie.

    2. handful.
       han'ful.
       hamful.

lm are sometimes for sound-softness, sundered by a vowel as

    E. elm, helm, overwhelm.
    D. elem, helem, overwhelem.

NUMBER.

The Dorset still owns a few nouns with the plural ending *en* for *s*:

    cheesen,   housen,   pleäçen,   vu'zen.
    cheeses,   houses,   places,   furzes.

The West Friesian holds many cases of this plural ending, which, indeed, in the Short Grammar of Japix is given as the usual ending for the plural of consonant-ended nouns.

In the West Friesian Gospel of St. Matthew we read
    'as scjippen midz yn di wolwen,'
    'as sheep-en midst in the wolv-en.'

    'hoedend as di slang-en, ind gol as di douwen,'
    'heeding as the snak-en, and harmless as the dov-en.'

    'Byn him hannen ind fuotten,' (Matt. 22).
    'Bind him hand-en and foot-en.'

en is mainly the ending of in New Friesic,
    'Di *foxen* hawwe *holen* ind di fuwgels hawwe *nesten*.'
                                 (Matt. viii. 20.)
    'The *foxen* have *holen* and the fowls have *nesten*.'

It is a pity that this *s* should have been taken, in a speech that hisses like our own, instead of the good liquid ending *en*, but this *s* will hold its place, and even take that of others, as especially that of *d* and *t*. It is found in the English verb ending *s* for *th*, as 'he writes' for 'he writeth,'

and in North Friesian
        Blees,   Fäihs,   hiehs.
        Blade,   food,   heath.

So in Cornoak *s* appears for the Welsh *d* or *dd*:

    W.   y tad,   y coed,   gorfyn y byd.
    Corn.   an tas,   an cois   gorfen an beys.
    E.   the father,   the wood,   end of the world.

The possessive case is in Dorset often given with of, o', instead of the case-ending -s, 'the veet o'n' for 'his feet,' though this form of case is mostly used in derision, as 'Look at the veet o'n,' 'Look at his feet' as something laughworthy.

TWO CLASSES OF THINGS.

Whereas Dorset men are laughed at for what is taken as their misuse of pronouns, yet the pronouns of true Dorset, are fitted to one of the finest outplannings of speech that I have found.

In Dorset-speech, things are offmarked into two classes:

1. Full shapen things, or things to which the Almighty or man has given a shape for an end; as a tree, or a tool: and such things may be called the Personal Class: as they have the pronouns that belong to man.

2. Unshapen quantities of stuff, or stuff not shapen up into a form fitted to an end: as water or dust: and the class of such things may be called the Impersonal Class, and have other pronouns than those of the personal class.

The personal pronoun of the personal class is HE, the objective case-form of which is EN, the worn form of the Saxon-English Accusative shape, *he-ene, hine, hin, en.* (Table 1.)

    S-E.   He araerde *hine* up.
    D.   He reared *en* up.
    S-E.   Petrus axode *hine*. (Mark c. 15.)
    D.   Peter axed *en*.

Thence it is said of western people that they make every thing *he*, but a tom-cat, which they call *she*.

It is markworthy that *en* is now the very form of this pronoun in the speech of Siebenburgen, or at least of Hermannstadt, in Transylvania, as I find in the song of Solomon, kindly given to me by H. H. Prince Lucien Bonaparte:

      éch saekt en, awer éch faand en nét.
    D. I sought en but I vound en not.

The personal pronoun for the impersonal class is *it*. We say of a tree 'he's a-cut down,' 'John vell'd en,' but of water we should say 'It's a-dried up.'

Again, the demonstrative pronouns for the personal class are *theäse* (hic) and *thik* (ille, is), and for the impersonal class we have *this* (hoc) and *that* (illud, id), so that we have four demonstrative pronouns against the Book English two. We should say

'Come under *theäse* tree by *this* water.'
'Teäke up *this* dowst in *theäse* barrow.'
'Goo under *thik* tree, an' zit on *that* grass.'
'Teake *thik* pick, an' bring a little o' *that* hay.'

If a woman had a piece of cloth she might say "*This* cloth is wide enough vor *theäse* teäble:" since, as long as it is unshapen into a table-cloth, it is impersonal; but as soon as she may have made it up into a table cloth, it belongs to the personal class: and then we should say of it:

Theäse or *thik* cloth do belong to
theäse or thik teäble.

If a right-speaking Dorset man were to say '*theäse* stwone' I should understand he meant a whole shapen stone, whereas '*this* stwone' would mean a lot of broken stone.

Of a brick bat he would say 'Teäke *en* up.'
Of a lot of brick-rubbish, 'Teäke *it* up.'
'*Thik* ground' would mean a field, but
'*That* ground' a piece of ground.

There is much seeming grammatical personification in our English version of the Bible, but we should not take the use of *his* for our *its*, to be always a token of personification.

The leviathan, the wild ass, the horse, and the raven, are given with the pronoun *he* in the book of Job, but we have in Mark 9 "if the salt have lost *his* saltness, wherewith will ye season *it*."

In Saxon-English we have "thys mihte beon geseald to miclum weorthe," (Matt. XXVI. 9). "This (ointment) might be sold for a great price," where thys is the neuter Dorset impersonal pronoun: whereas *sealf*, ointment, is feminine, but we should still, in Dorset, call it *this* not theäse, as a loose quantity of stuff.

Mr. Akerman writes me that in his part of Wiltshire, the cases which are marked among us by our *theäse* and *thik*, are shown by *thik* and *thuk*.

The word *thik* is the Saxon-English *tha-ylce* or *tha-ylc*, the Scotch, *the ilk*, and the old English *thulke*, which, in Chaucer's time, was shortened to *thilk*.

Thilke day that they were children,
D. *Thik* day that they wer childern.

And therof cometh rain-frost, as *thulke* mist doth fleo,
And thereof cometh rain-frost as that mist doth flee.
Lives of the Saints.

I have sometimes almost felt that we had three uses, instead of two, of our demonstrative pronouns: one for a near thing, *this, theäse*: one for a farther but outshown thing, *thik, that*; and a third for a farthest thing, or a thing not before the speaker, *yonder*.

The North Friesians may say:
De hirre buhm ás man; de dirre, dán; an janner, san.
The here tree (beam) is mine; the there, thine; and yonder, his.

So the Welsh, having these three kinds of pronouns, can say:
Mae yn rhaid i *hwn*, a *huna*, vyned at *hwnw*.

It is needful for *this* man (*here*) and *that* one (*there*) to go to *that* absent or farthermost (*yonder*) man.

The objective form of THEY is not THEM but is EM, the Saxon-English hym or him; HIM, HYM, HEM, EM:

Faeder, forgyf him (Luke XXIII. 34.)
Father, forgive them.

We find *hem* for *them* in the "Metrical Lives of the Saints," written in the time of King Edward I. and in "Sir John Maundeville's Travels," written soon afterwards, in the early part of the fourteenth century. In speaking of the Antipodes, it says "It semethe *hem*, that we ben under *hem*." In Dorset, "Do seem to em, that we be under em."

We can trace the Dorset *en* and *em*, the Anglo-Saxon *hine* and *hym*, to the Gothic, in which they are *ina* and *im*. "Andhôfun áuk jáinaim anahháitandam *im* (Dorset *em*), inthizei ni attaúhun *ina*," (Dorset *en*,) &c.: "But they answered *them*, asking why they had not brought *him*," &c. —*Gothic Homily*. The old personal pronouns *hem* and *her*, A-S. *him* and *hira*, for *them* and *their*, seem to have given place to the demonstrative ones *thæm* and *thæra*, of which *them* and *their* are worn shapes. Thus the Latin *hic* and *iste*, have been displaced by the Italian *questo* and *quello*.

When a pronoun in an objective case is emphatical, it is given in its nominative shape instead of its objective case. We should say, unemphatically, 'Gi'e me the pick,' or 'Gi'e en the knife,' or 'Gi'e us the wheat,' or 'Gi'e em their money;' but emphatically, Gie'e the money to *I*, not *he*; or 'to *we*,' not 'to *they*.' This is an analogous substitution to that of the emphatical dative case for the nominative in French; as 'Je n'irai pas, *moi*:' 'I myself shall not go.

I often hear people, (who would be angry at being told that they could not speak English,) uttering *me* in the place of the nominative *I*, as 'who would like a flower?' *Me* (should like one).

But so it is with our bretheren, the North Frieslanders, who say: 'Dat az më,' That is I (me).

NUMERALS.

woone,	zix,
two,	zeven or zebm,
dree,	aïght,
vowr,	nine,
vive,	ten.

The Dorset owns the Saxon-English wording 'This temple wæs getimbrod on six and feowertigum wintrum:' 'Theäse temple wer a-builded in six an' forty winters:' the lower digits being named before the higher ones: and with numeral pronouns of quantity the singular, instead of the plural form of the noun, has been much used in the west, as

Five foot six. — Two dozen and nine.
Five score. — Twenty pound.

Dorset, in violation of English Grammar, holds analogically right forms of the pronouns of *self*. We say

'He've a-hurt *hizzelf*,' (not himself,)

'The childern have a-tired *theirselves*,' (not themselves,)

and

My book, or self,	Our books, or selves,
Thy book, or self,	Your books, or selves,
His book, or self,	Their books, or selves.

If *self* is to be taken as a noun, the Dorset is right, and if *self* be a pronoun, with *I, thou, he*, &c., then those pronouns should be inflected, as they are in the Icelandic and Saxon.

Dorset retains more than the English of the *en*-tailed adjectives, as *wooden*, made of wood; *leatheren*, made of leather; *hornen*, made of horn; *peäpern*, made of paper; *hempen*, made of hemp; *ashen, elemen, woaken*, made of ash, elm, or oak.

This ending should be retained in English for the sake of distinction;

for a 'paper bag' is rightly a bag to put paper in, as a 'wood-house' is a house to put wood in: a bag made of paper is a '*papern* bag,' not a paper-bag; and a house built of wood is a '*wooden* house,' not a wood-house.

Our useful adjectives ending in *some*, German *sam*, as *quarrelsome, noisome*, equivalent to the Latin ones in *ax*, — *loqu-ax*, given to talking; or *bundus*, — *vaga-bundus*, given to wandering, naming the state of a noun likely or given to do an action, would have been well taken into the national speech from any folk speech in which they might be found, instead of those borrowed from the Latin; as *heedsome*, attentive; *winsome*, likely to win or captivate: *lovesome*, disposed to love; *blithesome*, disposed to be blithe; *fadesome, laughsome, runsome* (as mercury), *meltsome* (as butter or lead). *Winning* and *loving* are bad substitutes for *winsome* and *lovesome;* since *winsome* does not mean actually *winning* one, but likely to win one; and *lovesome* is not *amans*, but *amasius*.

The North Friesian owns many of these adjectives, as
        betanksaam, bethanksome, grateful.
        wirksaam, worksome, industrious.

In a case in which a positive degree with a possessive case is used in Dorsetshire for a superlative degree, its folk-speech matches with an idiom in Hindoostanee; as 'Bring the long pick, the *long* woone ov all,' instead of the *longest* of all,' like the Hindoostanee 'Yee sub-ka burra hai:' 'This is the great one of all,' for 'the greatest.'

VERBS.

The verb TO BE is, in Dorset and Anglo-Saxon,

Present Tense.

Dorset.	A.-Saxon.	Dorset.	A.-Saxon.
I be,	ic beo.	We be,	we beoth.
Thou bist,	thu byst.	You be,	ge beoth.
He is,	he is.	They be,	hi beoth.

Past Tense.

Dorset.	A.-Saxon.	Dorset.	A.-Saxon.
I wer,	ic wære.	We wer,	we waeron.
Thou werst,	thu wære.	You wer,	ge waeron.
He wer,	he wære.	They wer,	hi waeron.

The auxiliary verb *may* and *might* is, in Dorset, *mid*.

In negative expressions, the word *not*, after an auxiliary verb ending in *d* or *s*, becomes '*n*; as, I *could'n*, I could not; I *should'n*, I should not; I *would'n*, I would not; I *didd'n*, I *midd'n*, I *muss'n*,—I did not, I may not, I must not.

HAVE.

Present Tense.

I have, I've.	We have, We've.
Thou hast, Thou'st.	You have, You've.
He have, He've.	They have, They've.

Past Tense.

I had, I'd.	We had, We'd.
Thou hadst, Thou'dst.	You had, You'd.
He had, He'd.	They had, They'd.

Future Tense.

I shall have, shall've.	We shall have, shall've.
Thou shalt have.	You —
He shall have, shall've.	They —

BE.

Present Perfect.

I have, I've a-been, &c.

Past Perfect.

I had, I'd a-been, &c.

Future.

I shall have, I shall've a-been, &c.

TO MAKE.

Present Habitual.

I do* meäke.	We do meäke.
Thou dost meäke.	You do meäke.
He do meäke.	They do meäke.

* *do* unemphatical is pronounced as *de* in French.

The pronoun *it* is often left out before *do* as (It) do rain; (It) do grow; (It) do seem.

Present Actual.

I'm a-meäkèn, &c.

The affix *a-* in this tense form is not the same as the *a-* of the perfect participle, but it is the Saxon-English preposition *on* with the verbal noun.

    S.-E. Ic waes on huntinge.
    D.   I wer a-huntèn.

Aorist.

I meäde, &c.

Imperfect or Habitual.

I did meäke, &c.

We have, in Dorset, an aorist, and also an imperfect tense-form of repetition or continuation, like the Greek, Latin, Russian, Persian, and French Imperfect or Iterative, as offmarked from the Aorist, Semelfactive, or Preterite.

A boy said to me, in speaking of some days of very hard frost, "They *did break* the ice at night, and *did vind* it avroze ageän nex' mornèn." That is they *broke* and *found* several times. If they had *broken* and *found* only once, he would have said: "They *broke* the ice at night, an' *vound* it," &c.

    She *beät* the child, is *beat at some one time.*
    She *did beät* the child, is *was won't to beat.*

Whence came this use of *did* ?

Not from the book-Saxon-English, or Friesian. They have it not.

Not from the Normans. It is not found in old or modern French. From the Britons of the West ?

It may be, as Britons lived among the English, and we find, in Cornoak, a like use of *do* .

    "my a wra care." 'I do love.'

This imperfect tense-form is a great mark of south-western English, though, I think, it is missing in Devonshire, as it is in Northern English, but it holds again in Cornwall.

Chevalier Bunsen, however, once told H. H. Prince Lucien Bonaparte, that he had heard it with the verb *do* in Germany, and I think I have heard of its use in Saxony.

Imperfect Actual.

I wer a-meäkèn, &c.

Perfect Present.
I've a-meäde, &c.
Perfect Actual.
I've a-been a-meäkèn, &c.
Perfect Past.
I'd a-meäde, &c.
Perfect Past Actual.
I'd a-been a-meäkèn, &c.
Future.
I shall meäke, &c.
Future Actual.
I shall be a-meäkèn, &c.
Future Perfect.
I shall've a-meäde, &c.
or shall h'a-meäde, &c.

POTENTIAL MOOD.
Present or Aorist.
I mid meäke, &c.
Actual.
I mid be a-meäkèn, &c.
Present Perfect.
I mid've a-meäde, &c.
or mid ha' meäde, &c.
Actual.
I mid ha' been a-meäkèn, &c.

PASSIVE VOICE.
Present.
I be }
I'm } a-loved, or loved, &c.
Past.
I wer a-loved, or &c.
Present Perfect.
I've a-been a-loved, or &c.
Past Perfect.
I'd a-been a-loved, or &c.

Future.

I shall be a-loved, or &c.

Future Perfect.

I shall've a-been ⎫
   shall h'a-been ⎬ a-loved, &c.

POTENTIAL MOOD.

Present or Aorist.

I mid be a-loved, or loved, &c.

Perfect.

I mid've a-been ⎫
   mid h'a-been ⎬ a-loved, &c.

Jennings, in his Observations on the Western Dialects, says, "Another peculiarity is that of attaching to many of the common verbs in the infinitive mode, as well as to some other parts of different conjugations, the letter *y*. Thus it is very common to say, *I can't sewy, I can't nursy, he can't reapy, he can't sawy,* as well as *to sewy, to nursy, to reapy, to sawy,* &c.; but never, I think, without an auxiliary verb, or the sign of the infinite *to*." The truth is, that in the Dorset the verb takes *y* only when it is free, and never with an accusative case. We may say, 'Can ye zewy?' but never 'Wull ye zewy up theäse zêam?' 'Wull ye zew up theäse zêam?' would be good Dorset.

Belonging to this use of the free infinitive *y*-ended verbs, is another kindred one, the showing of a repetition or habit of doing, as

'How the dog do jumpy,' i. e. keep jumping. 'The child do like to whippy,' amuse himself with whipping. 'Idle chap, He'll do nothèn but vishy, (spend his time in fishing,) if you do leâve en alwone.' 'He do markety,' He usually attends market.

The Magyar language has both a form for the applied action, as *Iram*, and for the free action, as (*Irek*).

It seems a pity that we should have lost the free use of the affix *for* (off, or forth) in such words as *forgive, forswear.* The Friesians, like the

Germans with *ver*, make good use of it. They have many such words as

forlitten, to forlet, neglect;
forminderjen, to lessen off;
forlajngern, to forlong, or lengthen out;
forténnen, to forthin, or thin off or out;

and Japix, the Friesian poet, writes 'Hy forlear it sian fen't lan." He forlost, or lost off, the sight of the land, *forlear* being the verb of our participle forlorn.

Er-ended verbs are outekeing or frequentative verbs, as

beat, batter.	fret, fritter.
chat, chatter.	gleam, glimmer.
climb, clamber.	wind, wander.

The stem of the word *slumber* was marked in my Philological Grammar, p. 174, as wanting; though I knew it must be, or have been, somewhere in Teutonic speech; and I afterwards had the pleasure of finding it in Mr. Littledale's Craven version of Solomon's Song, kindly given me by H. H. Prince Lucien Bonaparte:

A *slaums*, bud mah hart wakkens,
I sleep, but my heart waketh.

We have a few of these *er*-ended words:

Blather, blether, to keep bleating.
Shatter, to shoot or cast about, as corn.
Happer, to keep hopping, as hail rebounding from the ground.

Many words which, in English, are strong or moulded, are in Dorset weak or unmoulded:

	English past tense.	*Dorset past tense.*
Blow,	blew,	blowed.
Build,	built,	builded.
Catch,	caught,	catched.
Crow,	crew,	crowed.
Draw,	drew,	drawed.
Gild,	gilt,	gilded.
Grow,	grew,	growed.
Hide,	hid,	hided.
Know,	knew,	knowed.
Run,	ran,	runned or rinned.
Slide,	slid,	slided.
Stride,	strode,	strided.
Throw,	threw,	drowed.

On the other hand, some verbs that are weak and mixed in English, are strong in Dorset :

climb, clomb. creep, crope. heave, hove. scrape, scrope.

It once seemed to me, that, as the Britons were much mingled with the English in Dorset, and as we Dorset men have therefore some British blood, the mingled thought of the English and Saxon mind in the West, might have taken the unmoulded tense-forms, from some such analogy, as we even now find will give unusual forms of words. I have heard a child, who had most likely learnt that his *zung* or *sung*, should be *sang*, take *brang*, as the past-tense of *bring*.

We need not think, however, as we see how unsettled these two classes of tense-forms are among the whole Teutonic race, that their use should be imputed to British or any other foreign thought.

The following few cases will show the unsettled state of the weak and strong verbs:

Bring	Brung, brang. *n.*	Pick	Puck. (*Hereford.*)
Climb	Clomb. *w.*	Quit	Quat. *n.*
Come	Cum'd. *n.*	Reach	Raught. (*Wilts.*)
Find	Fun. (*Lancas.*)	Rub	Rieb. (*German.*)
Fetch	Fot. (*Wilts.*) / Fotch. (*Hants.*)	Rise	Ruse. *n.*
		Scrape	Scrope. (*Dorset.*)
Give	Gov. *n.*	Shape	Shupe. (*O. English.*)
Heave	Hove. (*Hereford. and sailors.*)	Squeeze	Squoze. (*Hereford.*)
		Tell	Tell'd. (*Friesian.*) / Tell't. *n.*
Leap	Lap. *n.*		
Make	Maked. (*Friesian.*)	Take	Ta'ed. (*W. York.*)
Milk	Molk. (*German.*)		

The true Dorset retains, what one could wish the English had not lost, an affix or syllabic augment to the perfect participle, answering to one in the Saxon-English and German.

In German it is *ge-*, as

'Haben sie ge-funden das buch ?'

D. 'Have ye a-vound the book ?'

In Anglo-Saxon it is ge and also a and has become *a* in Dorsetshire; as 'He've Alost his hatchet.' 'She've Abroke the dish.'

A.-Saxon.—'Paulus GEbunden wearth GEsend to Rome.'— *Saxon Chron.* A. D. 50.

Dorset.—'Paul Abound wer Azent to Rome.'

A.-Saxon.—'Fela dwilda wæron GEsegen and GEheöred.'

Dorset.—'Many ghosts wer Azeed an' Ahierd.'

The augment or affix *ge*, by offwearing of the *g*, became *y* or *i* in the transition of the Saxon-English into our English; as in Yclep'd, called, from the Anglo-Saxon *clypian*, to call,—a word used by Milton:

"Come, thou goddess fair and free,
In heav'n Yclep'd Euphrosyne."—*L'Allegro.*

In a semi-Saxon poem, believed to be of the twelfth century, printed by Mr. Singer, the affix is almost constantly *i*; as

'—his deaz beoth *i*-gon;' 'his days are gone.'

'—thu weren *i*-freoed;' 'thou wert freed.'

'—ær thu beo *i*-brouht;' 'ere thou be brought.'

And in the works of Spenser we find the affix *y* in common use:

"She was Yclad,
All in silken camus, lily white."—*Spenser.*

In the legend of Saint Margaret, of the 13th century, edited by Mr. Cockayne, the affix *i*- is in full use, as it seems to have been in the time of Chaucer, who writes

'When Hector was *i*-brought all fresh *i*-slain.'
(*Knight's Tale.*)

D. 'When Hector wer *a*-brought all fresh a-slaïn.'

How much smoother is this line in old English or Dorset, than it is in our English,

'When Hector was brought all fresh slain"

with heaps of hard consonants unsundered by the vowel *i*- or *a*-,

-*ing*. the ending of the active participle and verbal noun is *èn*. It is markworthy that this ending -*ing*, which is truly English and Teutonic, is hardly any where -*ing* in Provincial speech. In the north it is mostly -*in* and -*an*, or *un* in other parts of England.

Dorset is, in many cases, more distinctive than our bookspeech, inasmuch as it has many pairs of words, against single ones of our books, and gives sundry sounds to other pairs, that, in English, are of the same sound; so that it withholds from the punster most of his chances of word-play.

'The people *told* the sexton and the sexton *toll'd* the bell' is in Dorset.

'The people *twold* the sex'on, an' the sex'on *toll'd* the bell.'

{ ale,	ail.		{ cane,	Cain.
{ eäl,	aïl.		{ ceäne,	Caïn.
{ board,	bor'd.		{ fall (verb),	fall (autumn).
{ bwoard,	bor'd.		{ vall,	fall.
{ breach,	breech.		{ foul,	fowl.
{ brêch (e=2	breech.		{ foul,	vowl.
{ hole,	whole.		{ sale,	sail.
{ hole,	hwole.		{ zeäle,	saïl.
{ home,	holm.		{ son,	sun.
{ hwome,	home.		{ son,	zun.
{ mare,	mayor.		{ firs,	furze.
{ meäre,	mayor.		{ virs,	vuzzen.
{ pale,	pail.			
{ peäle.	païl.			

That the Dorset is not indistinctive will be seen from a few

WORDS OF NIGH MEANINGS.

Tough.   Reämy.

A stick may be *tough*, when it will bend without breaking, but cheese or bread is *reämy* when it will reach out into stringiness without breaking off.

Reamy is elastic in the sense of reaching out, but not in that of shrinking back.

Bank.   Balk.

A *balk* is a strip of turf between *two* lawns, as those of an open corn field; a *bank* is a high ridge.

Blowsy.   Frouzy.

Blowsy is having the feace reddened by labor or heat. *Frouzy* is loosely clad; slack.

Bundle.　　　Lock.

A *bundle* of hay is a lot bound up; a *lock* is as much as can be taken up in the two arms.

Bush.　　　Wride.

A *wride* of hazel or wheat, is the lot of stems growing out of one root or one grain; a *bush* may be of many wrides.

Blackberry.　　　Dewberry.

The *dewberry* is a big kind of *blackberry*.

Burn.　　　Zweal.

To *zweal* is to singe.

Bloom.　　　Blooth.

Blooth is blossom collectively, or the state of blooming.

Bleat.　　　Blather.

To *blather*, blether, is to keep, *bleating*, or talking, loudly and foolishly.

Ceäre.　　　Ho.

To *ho* is to be uneasy for uncertainties of after time. 'Ne beo ge na hogiende.' Do not be ho-ing or anxious.

Chump.　　　Log.

A *chump* of wood, is a very short cutting, a *log* a longer one, or a length.

Chimney.　　　Tun.

The *tun* is only that part of the *chimney* that reaches above the roof.

Crack.　　　Craze.

To *craze* a dish, is to *crack* it a very little, so that it does not open.

Crow.　　　Croodle.

To *croodle* is to make little crowings, as a happy babe.

Cry.　　　Churm.
　　　　　　　Charm.

A *charm* is a mingled sound, as that of many children learning lessons aloud.

Cry(v).　　　Tooty.

To *tooty* is to weep with broken sounds.

Print.　　　Daps.

A *print* is a mark printed by a die or type. *Daps* is a likeness of thing so close as if it were printed with it. 'He is the very daps of his father.'

Deaf. Dunch.

Dunch is a little *deaf*; hard of hearing.

Faggot. Bavèn.

A *bavèn* is a bundle of long, *untrimmed*, boughs.

Flinders. Flankers.

Flankers are outflying bits of fire. *Flinders* are outflying bits, as of a hard body smashed.

Gift. Hansel.

A *handsel* is a hand-gift, a gift given from hand to hand. A house may be a *gift*, but not a *handsel*.

Gully. Brook.

A *gully* is a channel that takes surface water. A *brook* is a spring-head stream, running into a river.

Hackle. Rwof, roof.

A *hackle* is a small overhanging *roof*, as that of a bee-hive.

Hill. Knap.

A *knap*, cnaep, knob, is a small, low, *hill*. In Somerset it is a batch.

Hop. Hick.

To *hick* is to hop on one leg. A bird may hop, not hick, on both legs.

Hobble. Scraggle.

To *hobble* about is to go hoppingly. To *scraggle* about is to go with the limbs screwed out into queer shapes.

Job. Choor.

A *job* is one full piece of work. A *choor* (char) is a turn, as a weekly turn, at occasional work.

Linch. Lawn.
Linchet.

A *linch*, or *linchet*, is a flattened ledge, as of corn-ground by a hill-slope. A *lawn* is a strip of land in an open field, as formerly Fordington Field.

Lancet. Fleäm.

A *fleäm* is a lancet of arrowhead shape, for bleeding cattle.

Leävèns. Orts.

Orts are the leavings of hay, from cows fed afield.

Litter.   Laïter.

A *litter* of piglings is one bed or sow's breed of them. A *laïter* of eggs is all the eggs laid by a hen at one time, before sitting.

Leäse (Leäze).   Meäd.

A *meäd* is a mown field; a *leäze* is an unmown field, for the zummer run of stock.

Limp.   Sumple.

Limp is loose to bend. *Sumple* is yielding to pressure.

Marry.   Marry wi'.

To *marry*, as the clergyman. To *marry with*, as the man.

Moot.   Root.   More.

A *moot* is the bottom of the stem of a felled tree, with all its roots; a *root* is a single outreacher; and a *more* is a tap-root.

Musheroom.   Tusheroom.

A *tusheroom* is an unwholesome white fungus.

Mouldy.   Vinny.

A *vinny* cheese is one with blue fungus (fen), from damp, but a cheese may be *mouldy*, in a mouldy or crummy state without fenniness.

Muggy.   Hazy.

Muggy weather is that with the air mingled with mist or damp. *Hazy* is that with a covering of cloud.

Ment.   Mock.

To *ment* another is to show the likeness of his form or behaviour, in a good way. To *mock* is to do so in derision.
'He do *ment* his father.' He is very like his father.

Nitch.   Nicky.

A *nitch* of wood is a great cutting or faggot, carried home by hedgers at night. A *nicky* is a small cutting or bundle of sticks for lighting fires.

Nettled.   Angry.

Nettled is angry at something in which we cannot ourselves cast all blame on the speaker. Pricked to the heart.

Peäve.   Steän.

To *peäve* a yard is to ram down stone. A road may be *steäned*, not peäved, by only laying down gravel.

Poll.   Shroud.

To *poll* a tree is to cut down the whole head. To *shroud* it is to cut off its side boughs that it may grow up tall.

Plush, plash, plesh.   Fell.

To *fell* wood is to cut it off. To *plush* a hedge is to cut the wood-stems, half off; and lay them down, that their side sprouts may grow up.

Run.   Scote.

To *scote* is to shoot along close to the ground.

Reed.   Straw.

Reed is hulm reached out straight for thatching.

Shelter.   Lewth.

Shelter is a screening from something falling, as rain or hail. *Lewth* is a screening from cold wind.

Smoke.   Smeech.

A *smeech* is a smoke-like body of upsmitten dust.

Slit.   Slent.

A *slit* is an opening, it may be intentional, as in a hard body. A *slent* is an offtearing in cloth.

Spotted.   Sparked.

A *spotted* cow is one with roundish spots, a *sparked* one is one with longish pointed marks.

If you throw ink, plumb, on paper, you will make *spots*. If it be cast obliquely, it will make *sparks*.

Stitch.   Hile.

A *stitch* is a cone of sheaves set up with their heads in a point. A *hile* is a long rooflike pile of sheaves, with their heads in a ridge, and with a sheaf at each pinion end.

Stile.   Bars.
Sprack.   Spry.

A *sprack* man is one given to spring about; active: a *spry* man is one that spring or jump high or far.

Seat.   Settle.

A *settle* is or rather was a long seat with a high back, as a screen from door-draughts.

Skillèn.   Outhouse.

A *skillèn* is a roof with open sides, an *outhouse* would most likely be inclosed.

Zwell (swell).   Plim.

A bad hand may *swell*, when it is not wished that it may. Bacon may *plim* in boiling, as it should.

Storm.   Scud.

A *storm* is a rising of rain-bringing wind. A *scud* is a short down-shooting of rain, as a shower.

Stocky.   Puggy.

A *stocky* man is a short thick stiff-bodied one. A *puggy* man is a short corpulent or outswelling one.

Saucy.   Voreright (Foreright).

Saucy is speaking ones mind with offensive or intentional freedom. *Foreright* is talking or doing right on without thinking of the presences of others, or of consequences, but without an offensive will.

Tack.   Rack.

A *tack* is a shelf reaching out from a wall: a *rack* was a wooden frame fastened up under the floor over head.

Like, in Dorset, as in some other counties, qualifies an adjective. 'He's down-hearted *like*:' 'He is *rather* down-hearted.' 'He is all mwopèn *like*.' The adjective *like* (saa, sse, see,) is exactly so applied in Hindoostanee; as, Æk kaalaa-*saa* g'horaa:' 'A black-like horse; a rather black horse.'

The old speech of the West, will be holden for some time, as the language of the house, though the children may learn English, and speak it to their betters abroad; since, if a man comes home, with what his friends would call 'a clippèn ov his words,' a clipping of his words, or talkèn fine, it is only laughed at as an affectation of gentility. This will be understood by a case of which I was told in a parish in Dorset, where the lady of the house had taken a little boy into day-service, though he went home to sleep.

The lady had begun to correct his bad English, as she thought his Dorset was; and, at last, he said to her, weeping "There now. If you do meäke me talk so fine as that, they'll laef at me at hwome zoo, that I can't bide there."

A FEW DORSET EXPRESSIONS.

'The vu'st bird, the vu'st eäss.' The first bird, the first earthworm. The first come the first served.

Of deep alluvial soil, like that of Blackmore, it may be said in Johnsonian English. It is remunerative to the inhabitants, but inconvenient to travellers. In Dorset it might be shorter:

'Good vor the bider, bad vor the rider.'

We have a rather free use of *to*, as an adverb, meaning *to* rather than forward, *in* or *up* in union, rather than out or off from union, as 'zet to,' set yourself on the work. 'Put to;' Put the horses on to the waggon. 'Hold or Pull to;' Hold or pull in or up to you. He's a-took to;' He is taken a-back, or stopped in his course. 'Go to' of the Bible is our 'zet to.' Go at the work.

So in North Friesian 'tó,' an 'auf,' to an off, to and fro; 'jö döhr ás tó,' the door is to, i.e. shut, as in our shut to the door.'

Fall } Vall at } go, begin at.
Vall } Vall to }
      Vall in wi', coincide.
      Vall out, quarrel.

Give { Give, yield. 'The vrost do gi'e.' It begins to thaw.
Gi'e { Gi'e in, concede.
      Gi'e up, surrender.
      Gi'e on, Hand on.

Gifts, white spots on the finger nails.
        Gifts on the vinger
        Sure to linger,
        Gifts on the thumb
        Sure to come.

Put. Put out, make crabbed by adverse circumstances.
Put to, driven into a strait.
Put up, to take quarters, as at an inn.
Put up wi', to bear, endure, as trying the patience.
Put upon, imposed on.

Shrow-crop. The shrewmouse. The folklore of Dorset is that if it run over a man's foot, it will make him lame. Thence, in Hampshire, it is called the Overrunner.

Sluggard.
    Sluggard's guise,
    Lwoth to bed, an' lwoth to rise.

Spring months.
    March wull sarch, Eäpril wull try,
    Maÿ 'ull tell if you'll live or die.

Teäke } Teäke off, imitate, make a drawing of. 'He's a-
Take }   teäkèn off the church.'
Teäke after, be like in mind or body. 'He do teäke after his father.'

Whippence. Whoppence.
Half a groat, want two pence.
More kicks than halfpence.

INTENSITIVES.

A bangèn, brushèn, lincèn, or trimmèn, big heäre.

NUMBERS.

Nouns ending in S (15), or Z (16), or SH (17), or CH, or DGE (18), after another clipping, should all have, as some of them already have in the plural shape the ending ES or EN for S only, as

    copse,   copses.
    apse,   apses.
    adze,   adzes.
    axe, aks,   axes.
    kex, kecks,   kexes.

OF THE DORSET DIALECT.

    fox,   foxes.
    latch,   latches.
    match,   matches.

or

    copsen,
    apsen,
    adzen,
    axen,
    foxen,
    latchen,
    matchen.

Or with S before the other clipping, as

    hasp.
    chasm.
    cast.
    cask.

Anglo-Saxon and Dorset pronouns.

TABLE 1.

N. He (Masculine. He.)
G. His (he-es.)
D. Him (he-um.)   HIM (B. English.)
A. HINE (he-e-ne.)   Hin, Hen, EN (Dorset.)

TABLE 2.

N. Hit (he-t) Neuter, IT.
G. His (he-es.)
D. Him (he-um.)   IT.
A. Het (he-t) IT.

TABLE 3.

Plural. They.

N. Hi (he-e.)   THEY.
G. Hira, heora (he-e-ra.)   THEIR.
D. Him, heom (he-um.)   } HEM, EM. (Dorset.)
A. Hi (hi-e.)

TABLE 4.

THIS.

N. THES. THEOS. (THIS. THEASE.) (Dorset.)

Table 5.

Plural.

N. THAS,
G. THESSA, } THE'ASE.
D. THISS-UM. (THEASUM, THEASEM.) Dorset.

Table 6.

Pronoun for they, those.

Plural.

N. THA (thaè.)   THEY.
G. THARA (tha-e-ra.)   THEIR.
D. THAM (tha-um.) } THEM.
A. THA (tha-e.)

Whereas the Dorset EN stands for the bookspeech HIM, it is clear that the bookspeech has kept the Dative HIM ; and the Dorset the Anglo-Saxon HINE for both Dorset and Angol-Saxon.

Table 4.

THEASE, THEASUM, THIK.

Thease is seemingly a shape of the Saxon THES, THEOS (This).

Table 4.

And Theäsum of the Saxon Dissum (Theäse.)

Table 5.

In North Devon,
    Thick   is   this.
    Thak,   that.

THOSE.

For those the Dorset uses *THEY* as

They woaks be hollow
They cows be leän.

Ezekiel i. v. 10, "And *they* four had the face of an ox on the left side ; *they* four also had the face of an eagle."

    tha. ilk ; is from the Anglo-Saxon, *ylc, ealc, aelc.*
        Frs. *ellik, ek.*

Meaning each, the single one, *tha-ylc.* The single body not the quantity of stuff.

Unlike the Anglo-Saxon which has Ge (ye), for the nomiative, and eow (you), for the objective case, the Dorset has you for the nominative and ye for the objective, you. However, you is given for ye for an offmarking of some from others, as

>I twold *ye* o't.
>
>I told *you* of it.
>
>{ I twold *you* if
>
> "I didd'en tell *others* o't."

"*You*" *as a Nominative.*—"A writer says," in the Homilies contained in the Trinity College, Cambridge, MS. B 14, 52, "we have, I think, the earliest instance of *you* as a nominative. As it is limited to the imperative mood, the blunder, if it be one, may have arisen from the writer looking upon the pronoun following a transitive verb as an accusative. The same mistake has been committed by some recent grammarians, who take *ye* as an accusative or objective case in the biblical phrase, "Comfort *ye*, comfort *ye* my people." In the first set of extracts, *ge=ye*, the correct form, is employed after the imperatīve plural; in the second set, *giu=you* is used:—1. *Venite benedicti*, &c., Cumeth *ge* ibletsede; *Ite maledicti*, &c., Witeth *ge* awariede gastes. (O. E. Homilies, 2nd Series, p. 5.) 2. *Convertimini ad me*, &c., turneth *giu* to me. (Ib. p. 59). *Convertimini ad me, et ego convertar ad vos*, turneth *giu* to me, & ich will turne me to *giu*. (Ib. p. 61). In the following example, *geu* may stand for *ge* or *giu: Lavamini, mundi estote,* wasseth *geu* and wunieth clene (Ib. p. 17.)

DO.

Commonly used as a helping word to time-words of the present time, as

>I do write.
>
>He do read.
>
>We do hear.
>
>They do zae.

Was formerly so used in book-English, and is found here and there in our authorised English Bible, and in the Prayer Book.

>"All the world *doth* worship Thee."
>
>   *Te Deum.*

"Fishes *do* multiply."
Prayer.

"We *do* now most justly suffer."
Prayer in the Time of Dearth.

"We *do* give Thee most humble and hearty thanks."
Thanksgiving.

"We *do* earnestly repent."
Confession.

"Ye that *do* truly and earnestly repent you."
Exhortation.

"*Didst* safely lead thy people."
Baptism.

   John III. 17.
   Acts VII. 51.
   Luke XVII. 27, 28.

"We do give Thee."

"All they that do confess."
Thanksgiving.

And in an old *Grammaire Angloise è Francaise*—

Tu vois.	Thou *doest* see.
Il void.	He *doth* see.
Nous voyons.	We doe see.
Vous voyés.	Ye doe see.
Ils voyent.	They do see.
We.	*Nous.*
You, *ou* Ye.	*Vous.*
They.	*Ils.*
Et terminent la seconde personne singuliere de leurs verbes en St.	And they do ende the second person singulier of their verbes in *st*.

Did is used to mark, ofttimes instead of one time of a doing, as—

He went to town on Monday (once).

He did goo to town every Monday (many times).

The past tense of Dig is digged, as it surely ought to be in English, and is in
   2 Kings xix. 24.
   Isaiah v. 6.

Dig is the only ig-ended verb that is moulded in English.

D.

Hide,	hided.
Slide,	slided.
Stride,	struded.

TCH.

Catch. catched.

Catch, is the only TCH-ended verb that is moulded in English.

Blowed.
Crowed.
Drawed.
Growed.
Knowed.
Throwed.

In which the folk-speech follows the pattern of

Bow,	glow.
Claw,	low.
Flow,	paw.
See,	zee'd.
Give,	gi'e, gied.

L. D.

Build,	builded.
Gild,	gilded.

R.N.

Burn,	burned.
Learn,	learned.

As in the Bible and as others in English.

In time-words of one breath-sound and ending in en, the n is mostly left out.

A-bore.
A-broke.
A-drove.
A-vroze.
A-rod.
A-shore.

A-spoke.
A-stole.
A-zwore.
A-trod.
A-wore.

Some one-sounded and moulded ones take ed.

A-drawed.
A-growed.
A-knowed.
A-drowed.

The fore-wordling *a* was carried over to the Barony of Forth, in Wexford, by the West English followers of Strongbow, under Henry II., where, as in Dorset, the n for en as an ending particle of a short verb is left out, as

Abore,	borne.
Ashore,	shown.
Awore,	worn.
Atore,	torn.
A-wrote,	written.

Our ago, for gone, is one of such forms.

A for the old Saxon *an*, meaning in or *on*, is put to verbs nouns, as

"Daddy's gone a-huntèn," or
He's a-ploughèn, a-zowèn, a-reapèn, a-mowèn.

Causing of Time-taking:

For a causing of a time-taking, make, meäke is mostly used; as

The bwoy won't do what he is abid.
I'd meäke en do it.

For the causing of a time-taking to a time giving, have is often used as,

"He had a house builded."
"He caused a house to be builded."
"He had the tree a-velled."

NOT.

The word not, after some of the helping verbs, often loses the o and sometimes the t also, as

> I ben't.
> I wern't or werdn'.
> I can't.
> I couldn'.
> I coodn'.
> I won't.
> I woudn'.
> I midn'.
> I shan't, shont'.
> I shouldn'.
> I don't.
> I didn'.
> I mus'n.

Some time-words which are weak and unmoulded in English are strong or moulded in Dorset, as

> I crope.
> He clomb.
> She scrope.

A little girl in a Sunday school said to a teacher—

"There, Jim (her brother) have a-scrope out the p vrom 'psalm' an have a-meäde such a muddle in his book."

Jim answered, "Well, what if I have a-scrope out the p, what wer the good o'n, 'e didden spell anything, did 'e?"

One cannot readily tell whether the Dorset or the Queen's English sins most in these weak and strong shapes of the time-words.

The Dorset   Crope,   Clomb,

are justified by the Anglo-Saxon and Teutonic shaping of time-words, but

> Blowed for blew.
> Crowed,   crew.

Drow'd, threw.
Growed, grew.
Knowed, knew.

have not followed the Saxon. Though again the English, along with Dorset, has given the weak shape of the past time for the strong one. One sample will show what is meant:

We say,—
> He glided.
> He glád. (Saxons.)

We say,—
> He griped. King Alfred would have said,
> He gráp.

Word shortening and wordwear.

English words have been shortened from their Anglo-Saxon forms by the out-leaving of breath-pennings and voicings, so some Dorset words are shortened from their book English forms.

The Dorset has more freedom than has the more straitly bound book-speech in the out-casting or keeping of clippings, so that for the sake of smoothness or shortness we may leave them out or keep them in. We may say—

> A lot o' sheep, or
> A half of an apple.
> The ground is green, or
> The groun' mid be wet.
> Ha-skim cheese, or
> Half-skim cheese.
> A cheese lö't, or
> A cheese loft.
> All o't, or all ov'it,
> All o'm, or all ov em.
> Lets or le'ss play rounders.
> Better 'n that, or
> Better than that.

A GLOSSARY

OF THE

DORSET DIALECT OF THE ENGLISH LANGUAGE.

ABBREVIATIONS.

A.S.	Anglo-Saxon.	Ger.	German.	Sco.	Scotch.
Da.	Danish.	Go.	Gothic.	S.	South.
Du.	Dutch.	Gr.	Greek.	Swe.	Swedish.
E.	East.	Lat.	Latin.	Ir.	Irish.
Fr.	French.	N.	Northern Eng.	W.	West.
Frs.	Friesic.	O.E.	Old English.		

A.

ABOUT OV, About of. About often takes *of* after it, as "About ov an hour agoo," "About ov two eäcres o' groun'." This wording is true to the first meaning of the Saxon *anbutan*; About, which means on the out-side, and the wording matches also the French *autour de*.

A-COTHED. Rotten or diseased in the liver, as sheep with the plaice. (A.S.) Cothe; "swilc cothe com on mannum." "Such an ailing came on men."

AFEARD, 'afeärd,' and 'afraid', are truly two sundry words; 'afeärd' is only smitten with fear, and 'afraid' is frayed or scared away, driven, it may be in fear, fro or from.

A-FEARD. Affrighted; afraid.

AGEAN, Agien. Against.

AGGY (E.) Cornery with sharp looking joints, as a very thin man. Agg (Saxon ecg) means an edge, or point, or corner.
Dorset readily takes thing-names and uses them as time-words, as they are; or with the ending *y*.

AGGY (E.) To gather eggs, such as pheasants' eggs, in the laying season. Boughy: To cut boughs. Coochy: To pick couch. Copsy: To cut tufts and thistles in fields.

AHWOLE. A-whole; in a whole state. "I should like to die awhole," that is not in pieces, as in a smash on the railway.

AIRMOUSE (E.) The bat.

AIR VLEES (E.) Air flies. Flies that seldom pitch from hovering in the air.

AISH. The ash.

A-LASS'N. Lest.

ALIK'. Like, Alike.

AL'S. All this. "Al's day:" "All this day."

ALLER. The alder tree.

AMPER. Pustules, or the matter of them. "The chile is all out in an *amper*."

ANBY. At a near time; soon; by-and-by.

ANEWST, OR ANISTE. At nearest. "*Anewst* the seäme;" "Very nearly the same." "Don't goo *aniste* en." Don't go near him.

ANIGH (Saxon, an-neah). Near to.

ANKLY. The ankle.

ANNAN. A word used as in the sense of "What did you say?"

ANY-WHEN. At any time.

A-PIGGY-BACK, A-pig-a-back, A-pack-a-back. A mode of carrying a child on one's back, with his legs under one's arms and his arms round one's neck.

A-PISTY-POLL. A mode of carrying a child with his legs on one's shoulders and his arms round one's neck or forehead.

APPLEMEAT (E.) Any dough food with apple in it.

A'RA. Ever a. "Have ye a met *a'ra* bwoy wi' a dog?" "He zent a cherry without *a'ra* stwone."—*Old Rhime*.

ARCHET. Orchard.

ARG. To argue.

ARN. A contraction of "e'er one;" ever-one.

ASH-CANDLES. The seed-vessels of the ash tree.

ASKER. A water eft.

A-STROUT. Stretched out stiffly, like frozen linen.

A-STOODED. Sunk (as waggon wheels) into the ground.

A-STOGGED. Having one's feet stuck into clay or dirt.

AT. To play at, or have at; to contend with, or take or meet in a game or otherwise. "We dree'll at you dree."

ATHIRT. Athwart, across.

AUVERLOOK. To overlook; to bewitch or look upon with the "evil eye."

AUVERRIGHT. Opposite; right over against.

AVORE. Before: "We synd her ætforan the." "We are here before thee."—*Ælfric's Dialogue*.

A-VRORE. Frozen. (A.S. and Ger. ge-froren.) "So cold that he al i-frore beo."—*Metrical Lives of Saints*.

AWAKED. Awake.

AX. (A.S. axian.) To ask.
"Hi ne dorston axian." "They durst not ask."—*Luke ix. 45*.
"A question wold y axe of you."—*Duke of Orleans' Poems*.

AXANHOLE. An ash-hole, or a place to stow wood-ashes in.

A-ZET. Set, or planted.

A-ZEW. Dry of milk; no longer giving suck. "The cow's a-zew." (A.S. on sew.)

B

BACKHACK (W.) To beat abroad clods afield with a mallet.

BACKHOUSE. An outhouse, a woodhouse.

BACKSIDE. The back yard of a house.

BAD. Used often for sick or ill. How's John? O, very bad.

BAFFLE. To frustrate, to baulk.

BALLYWRAG, or Ballawrag. To scold or accuse in foul language. (A.S. wregan.) To accuse.

BANDY. A long heavy stick with a bent end, used to beat abroad dung in the fields.

BANDY-LAGS. Crooked legs, or one having crooked legs, as if like a bandy.

BANGEN, Banging. Used as an intensitive; as a "bangèn girt apple."

BANKROUT. A Bankrupt. "The *bankrout's* banquet, which

done, the diuell, falling sicke, makes his last will and testament, this present yeare 1613, by Thomas Dekkar." 1613, black letter, 4to.—Book catalogue.

BARERIDGE. To ride bareridge is to ride on the bare back of a horse without a saddle.

BARGE. The line of small pieces of tile or thin stone let into a wall over the touch-line of a roof built against it so as to keep rain out of the joint.

BARGEN. A small farm or homestead.

BARKEN. A grange yard; a barton.

BARLEY-BREECH, or Breach. "Barley-break. A game of catching played by six. The catchers stood in the middle on ground called Hell." Palgrove's Herrick, p. 3, No. 122. [I have seen it played with one catcher, on hands and knees, in the small ring (Hell), and the others dancing round the ring crying, "Burn the wold witch you Barley-breech."

BARLEY-BIRD. The wryneck.

BARM. Yeast.

BARNABY BRIGHT. "The longest day, an' the shortest night." Said of St. Barnabas-day, about the summer solstice.

BARROW PIG. A hog, not a sow.

BARTON. Same as barken.

BATCH (West and Somerset). A hillock, a small rising of the ground, a knap. "The defendants then went across to a batch in the field and began to ferret it."—Dorset paper.

BAVEN. A faggot of long untrimmed branches of wood.

BAY. A bank across a stream; a space between the beams of a barn.

BEA'NHAN,' (bear in hand). To think or hold an opinion; to maintain.

BEACONWEED. The plant goosefoot (*chenopodium*).

BEAS. Beasts; applied only to neat cattle.

BEAVER of a hedge. The bushes or underwood growing out on the ditchless side of a single hedge; or the greensward beside the beaten road in a lane.

BECALL. To call by bad names.

BEDWINE. Traveller's joy (*clematis vitalba*).

BEENS. Because. "I can't do it to-day, *beèns* I must goo to town."

BEEPOT. The strawen house for a swarm of bees. The beehive,

as it may differ from the beepot, would, I think, be the pot with its hackle and stand.

BEETLE-HEAD. The bull-head, or miller's thumb (*cottus gobio*). E. The tadpole.

BEKNOWN. Known about : a good word as differing in meaning from *known*. If a know John from other men, he is *known* to me. If I do not know *about* some deed of his, it is *unbeknown* to me.

BELLY. A bundle of thatch, not reed.

BELL-PLOW. A waggon with a team of belled horses.

BENNETS. The stems and flower heads of grass.

"He cared not for dint of sword or speere,
No more than for the stroke of straws or bents."

BERGIE (Frs.), Beorgan (S)., Barge. To cover, shield. The barge (boat) may be so called as being covered or roofed.

BETTERMOST. Best, as of the best kind. "Bettermost vo'k."

BIBBER. To shake as with cold.

BIDE. To dwell, abide, or stay. (A.S. Bid an.)

BIDDLE, Bittle. A beetle; the tool.

BIE. A bolster case.

BIRD-BATTEN. The catching of birds by night with a net. Bird-batting is described by Fielding in the tenth chapter of his "Joseph Andrews."

BIRD-KIPPY. To keep birds from corn.

BIRDPEARS. Haws.

BISSEN. Bist not; art not.

BIT AN' CRIMP. Every bit an' crimp; every particle of anything.

BIT AN' DRAP. A bit of food and a drop of drink.

BIVER. To shake or quiver, as with cold or fear. To bibber which see.

BLACK-BOB. The cockroach (*blatta orientalis*).

BLACK JACK. The caterpillar of the turnip-fly (*athalia spinarum*).

BLATCH. Black stuff or soot.

BLATHER. A bladder.

BLAVER. The black pollack.

BLEAME OFF. To impute the blame which lies on one's self to another.

BLEARE. To low as a cow; or to cry loud as a fretful child.

BLETHER. To bleat or blare much; to talk noisily.

BLINE-BUCK-O'-DEAVY. Blindman's buff. Blind buck. The Friesians give the name 'bokke' (buck) to the beginner, or main player, for the time, in their children's games. The word 'buff' in "Blind man's buff" may mean the 'buff' or 'buffet' given to the buck by a player.

BLIT. Blighty.

BLOODYWARRIORS. The garden wall-flower (*cheiranthus cheiri.*)

BLOOTH, or Blowth. The blossom of fruit trees collectively.

BLOOENS. Blowings; blossoms, singly.

BLOOM, BLOOMS, } A feverish flush on the cheeks.

BLOSSOMS. Snowflakes.

BLOW. To tell upon one.

BLUE-VINNY, or vinnied, cheese. Blue mouldy. The Dorset blue vinny cheese is made from milk twice skimmed.

BODKINS. (*See* Wey).

BOLD. Plump. "Good bold seed."

BOLT. To run to seed ere its time. Spoken of worts.

BOLT (of Willows). A bundle of willows of given tale, peeled, and fit for the basketmaker.

BONCE. A stone ball; a very large marble.

BONK. (W.) A bank.

BOOK O' CLOTHES. A wash of clothes; the linen of one washing.

BORIS-NORIS. Going on blindly, without any thought of risk or decency.

BOTTOM. Steadfast-mindedness or principle. "There's noo bottom to en."

BOTHERUM, or Botherem. The yellow ox-eye; corn marygold (*chrysanthemum segetum.*)

BOY'S-LOVE. The herb southern-wood.

BRACK. A breach.

BRAGS. Boastings. "To make oone's brags;" "To boast."

BRAID. To wreathe, twine, plat. "I'll bräïd a vishèn line wi' this ho'ss heäir."

BRANTEN. Bold; impudent.

BRANDIS (E.) A brandiron.

BRASSEN. Made of brass.

BRAWLER. A bundle of straw, as brushwood faggots, in which the straws or wood brangles or brawls about, instead of lying straightly even, as reed drawn.

BREAST-PLOUGH. A turfcutting tool.

BREDE (W). To braid.

BREAK. To break; to fail in business. "Mr. Chapman's a-broke."

BREMBLE, Brimble. A bramble.

BREZE, Breeze, Braze (W). To press, push down.

BRICKLY OR BRUCKLY. Brittle, "How bruckly this bread is." "Though we be more brickle than glasse."—*Bisse's Sermon at Saint Paul's,* 1508.

BRICKMAKING at Broadmayne. The work begins by the heading of the clay or taking off of the top soil. The clay is dug mostly in the winter months and cast back loosely or wheeled back into a heap to soak for the coming season of brickmaking, which begins about March or the beginning of April. The clay is worked (tempered) in a pugmill, turned by a horse or donkey, or trodden by men's naked feet. The new-made bricks are wheeled to the drying ground on long barrows, and placed in rows (hacks), and when dry enough sent to the kiln. It takes two or three days to burn the bricks and about as long to cool them.

BRIMWARD. The same as borrid, or boarward: "cùm vere calor redit ossibus."

BRING-GWAIN. To bring one going; to bring one on one's way. The Yorkshire folk-speech has *to set* for it; and the Scotch *to convoy*, as in a Kelso convoy; a stride and a half owre the doorstane. "I pray you, my lord, to commune with him, whiles I *bring* my Lord of Durham *going*."

BROADGRASS. The common red clover.

BROADWEED. The cow parsenip. "Heracleum Sphondilium" gathered for stypigs.

BROCKS. Broken pieces as of bread. "There's nothén a-left but brocks."

BROCKS (Frs.) "Bitten ind brokken." "Bits and brocks."

BROCKLE. Breaksome; apt to break out of field. Applied to cattle.

BRON, Bran, or Backbron, Backbran. A brand; a big log of wood put on at the back of the fire.

BRONDS (E.) An iron stand for a cooking vessel over a turf fire; a brand iron.

BROU, Brow (E.) Brittle.

BROW of a hedge. Brushwood overhanging a ditch, or bank.

BROWNSHELL-NUT. A kind of brown-rinded apple.

BROWSE. Brushwood twigs.

BRUCKLE. A quantity of broken pieces of rock, or other hard stuff.

BRUFF. Brittle—used in West Dorset.

BRUSHET. Brushwood, scrub. "He often cut brushet between the watercourse and the ledge."—Dorset paper.

BRUSHEN. An intensitive of size; as, "a brushèn great rat."

BRYANSTONE-BUCK. The stag-beetle (*lucanus cervus*), so called from being often found in the neighbourhood of Bryanstone.

BUCK (E.) A book or washing of clothes.

BUCKY. Stringy and tart. Said of cheese.

BUDGET. A leathern pouch, in which a mower carries his whetstone.

BUFF, Butt (N.E.) A clashing or bumping or a hitting together. "I met en vull butt or vull buff." I met him full clash in his very line of walk. From buff comes buffer.

BUG-A-LUG (E.) An effigy, a bugbear. A scarecrow or gallybagger. It means a bug or bugbear on a pole; a-lug meaning on a lug or pole.

BUMBLE, Bunnen. A sea fish, the smaller kind of conner.

BUN UP. To bunch or bend, or coil up, as a hedgehog or rabbit. Whence bunny, a rabbit.

BUNDLE. To bound quickly. "He bundled off." Took himself off suddenly or quickly. The word is used with a like meaning in Lincolnshire.

BUNT. To butt weakly, as a lamb.

BUOILEN. Boiling; the whole set or lot. "I'd hike out the whole buoilèn ò'm."

BURN-BEAT, or Burn-Beäke. To cut up and burn turf, and dress the ground with the ashes.

BEATBARROW (West Cornwall.) A heap of burnt turves.

BURR. A kind of stone, as Purbeck burr. Also a whetstone made of it.

BUSGINS. Buskins; short gaiters.

BUTTER AN' AGGS. Yellow toad flax (*Linaria vulgaris*), and narcissus.

BUTTER-DEAISY. The great white ox-eye.
BUTT. (*See* Buff.)
BUTTON (E.), Button-crawler (N.) The woodlouse.
BWEIL. Boil.
BWEITLE-HEAD (S.) The tadpole.
BY AN' BY. Soon.

C.

CADDLE. Entanglement; muddle.
CAG. To surfeit; cloy, clog.
CAG-MAG. Bad flesh meat.
CALL. Need; necessity.
CALL HWOME. To call in church; to call banns.
CAMMICK (A.S. camoc.) The plant restharrow (*ononis arvensis*).
CAMMISH. Scram, awkward.
CAPPLE COW. A cow with a white muzzle. (A.S. ceafl, a muzzle).
CAPSHEAF. A small sheaf of straw forming the tip of a thatched rick.
CAR. To carry.
CAS'N. Can'st not.
CAT. A small cutting of stick.
CAT. A clay-cat; a clay-stone.
CAX (E.) A kex.
CAXHEAD. The dry head of the wild carrot or other such wort.
CEARDS. Cards; wire-faced tools to card wool.
CHADEN. Chawdon; inwards of a calf.
CHAM, or Champ. To chew or champ.
CHAMMER. Chamber; bedroom.
CHANKER. A wide chink.
CHANKS. The under part of a pig's head.
CHARM (A.S. cyrm.) A noise or confusion of voices, as of children or birds. "Synnigra cyrm:" "The chyrm of sinners."
CHARM. Bed-charm. The writer when a child, was taught a bed-charm, comprehending the one given by Hone in his "Year-book," Dec. 18.

"Matthew, Mark, Luke, an' John,
Be blest the bed that I lie on;

> Vow'r carners to my bed,
> Vow'r anngels all a-spread;
> Oone at head an' oone at veet,
> An' two to keep my soul asleep."

CHATTERMAG. A chattering magpie; a chatterbox; a much talking woman.

CHAW (A.S. caw-an). To chew.

CHAWLY-WHIST (E.) Ashamed.

CHEAT. Bearded darnel (*lolium temulentum*).

CHEAT. Wild oats, or oats which, from lack of soil or food or other causes, have degenerated almost into the wild form, more like rye than oats.

CHEATERY. Cheating behaviour.

CHEEM. To chime.

CHEESE. A bag or pile of pummice from the cider wring.

CHEESE-LO'T, or Cheese-lote. A cheese loft or floor to dry cheese on.

CHEESECUTTER. A cap with a straight peak.

CHEESE-EATER. The tomtit, so called from its cry.

CHEESE STEAN (N.) A cheese stwone, a stone for a weight in a cheese wring.

CHEESE WRING. A cheese press.

CHETLENS, or Chetterlens. The entrails of a pig, cleaned and twined up in knots. Also a frill formerly worn on the bosom of shirts, and so called from its likeness to chitterlings.

CHETTEN. To kitten.

CHILVER. A ewe lamb. (A.S. cilferlamb).

CHILLDAG. A chillblain.

CHIMCHEAY (W.) A mincing talk; hamchaw.

CHIMLEY. A chimney.

CHIMP. A young shoot, as of a potatoe. To pick off chimps.

CHINE. The groove in the staves of a cask for the head.

CHINE (A.S. cyne, a chink.) "Ic ge-séah áne lytle cynan."
King Alfred's Boëtius.

CHIPEN (chipm). Made of chip or straw. "Gi'e me my chipm brimmer." Straw hat.

CHISOM. To germinate or throw out chimps, as potatoes in the spring.

CHOCK. A part of a neck of veal; to choke.

CHOCK-VULL. Choke full; full to choking.

CHOCK-DOG. An epithet bestowed, with more humour than complacency, on hard Dorset cheese.

CHOOR. A chare or job of household work done by an occasional or charwomen.

CHOOR, Chare, is from A.S. cer. cyre, a turn, as of time, a round coming, an occasion. "He het æt suman cyre onbærnen Rome byrig." "He had at some time or occasion, to burn Rome."

CHUBBY. Round, or full cheeked. "He's a chubby bwoy."

CHUCK. To toss anything underhanded. Also a word used in calling pigs.

CHUCKS (of wheat). Pinched grains in the husk.

CHUCKLE-HEAD. A dolt with a head as it were like a chuck or chump of wood.

CHUNK. Chump of wood; a big cutting or chip; as "a chunk of wood."

CIDER-WRING. A cider-press.

CLACKER, or Bird-clacker. A kind of rattle to frighten away birds from a corn field.

CLAPGEATE. A little gate that swings between two posts on which it is clapped or clashed by people who go round its head.

CLAPPERS. Fox earths.

CLAVY. A mantel-piece.

CLAY-CAT. A kind of roundish stone found in clay.

CLEANSHEAF (W.) Clearly; thoroughly.

CLEAR. Very or quite close. "How vur did ye goo?" "Clear into town."

CLEDEN, Clydern. Goosegrass (*galium aparine*.) Called also cleavers, clavers, or clivers, from their cleaving to bodies.

CLEVER. Clear. "Clever auver."

CLIM'; past tense, Clumb. "Clumben upp to the stepel."
Sax. Chron. 1070.

CLINKER. An icicle.

CLINT. To clinch a nail; and figuratively to complete one joke or exaggeration by another out-doing it.

CLIPS. To clasp between the thumb and fingers, or to fathom between the two arms. "I can clips thik tree."

CLIPSE (E.) To outdo some deed of another. "Can ye clipse that?" To clasp.

CLITPOLL. Having curled or tangled hair on one's poll or head.

CLITTY. Stringy and sticky; tangled in clods or lumps.

CLOCK. A dor-beetle.

CLODGY, Cludgy. Close; dumplike.

CLOG. A wooden bow at one head of a hay-rope, or a block at the end of a halter for tying a horse to a manger.

CLOT. A clod.

CLOTE. The yellow water lily (*nuphar lutea*).

CLOUT. A blow with the flat hand. "I'll gi'e thee a clout in the head."

CLUM. To clutch roughly or clumsily.

CLUMPER. A lump. "A clumper of gingerbread."

CLUTTER. A clatter. A loud clating or clashing, as of hard bodies.

CLUOSE. A close, very common in the name of fields, as Bushy Cluose, Long Cluose.

COCKLE, or more commonly called Cuckle. The burr of the burdock (*arctium*).

COCKLE. A knot or bow as from a catch in thread or twine in the unwinding of it.

COD. A pod or legume; as a bean-cod, or peas-cod.
"Dá gewilnode he is wambe gefyllan of tham beán-coddum."
—*Luke* xv. 16.

CODDLE. A hook, sometimes found in old open chimneys to hang the pot on.

CODGLOVES. Hedgers' gloves, with a bag for all of the fingers together.

COLE or Coll. To take one fondly round the neck. "To coll the lovely neck."—*Ovid's Metamorphosis.*

COLEPEXY. To glean the few apples that may be left on the trees after the crop has been taken in.

COLT. Footing; a novitiate's fine. "Ya must pây yer colt."

COME. To be ripe. "The pears ben't quite a-come."

COME o' To come of; to be altered from a state. "She wer pirty oonce, but she's finely a-come ö't."

CONKER. The fruit or hep of the wild rose; the single or "canker" rose.

CONKER. "I had rather be a canker in a hedge, than a rose in his grace."—*Much Ado about Nothing.*

CONNERS. Groundfish, rife by shores with a rocky bottom.

CONTRAPTION. A contrivance.

COOCOO'S BREAD. Wood sorrel.

COOCH. Couch grass; quitch-grass; creeping wheat-grass (*triticum repens*).

COOCHY. To work at picking of couch.

COPSE, Cops. A thick head of sprouts or shoots or tufts of grass. "The greens be all out in a copse."

COPSY. To cut off copses of rank grass or weeds in a summer lease.

CORE OF A RICK. The middle of it when it has been cut away all round.

CORNISH JACK. The Cornish chough (*corvus graculus*).

COTHE (A.S. Cotha, Cothe). An ailing. "Swilk cothe com on mannum." "Such an ailing came on man."—*Chron.* 1087. A disease of sheep, the plaice worm in the stomach. (*See* Floor.)

COUNT. To reckon; to guess.

COWLEASE. An unmown field; a summer grassfield.

COW-BEABY. A boy or girl childishly meek-hearted, or mother-sick.

COW-CAP. A metal knob put on the tip of a cow's horn.

COWHEART. A coward.

COWS AND CA'VES. Lords and ladies. The barren and fertile flowers of the *arum*.

CRAMMET (W.) An afternoon lunch. (*See* Dewbit.)

CRANNICK. A root of furze, or stool of a furze bush.

CRAVEL. A mantel-piece; sometimes called "the clavy."

CRAWLY-WHISHT. (*See* "Chawly-whisht.")

CRAZE. To crack a little.

CREEZE. Dainty; taffety.

CREWEL (W.) A cowslip.

CRIB. To hook in slyly, or by little and little; to pilfer.

CRICK. To hurt the neck or backbone by a sudden and hard crooking or wrenching of it. A creek.

CRICKET. A low stool for a child.

CRIMP. A little crumb.

CRIMS. Cold shivers, or the creeping of the flesh, of which folks speak in the wording, "It made my flesh creep."

CRIPS (W.) Crisp.

CRIP OFF. As to crip off a flower by a short bending with a pinching of the stalk.

CRIPNER. A crupper.

CRIPPLEISH. Like a cripple; rather lame.

CRISS-CROSS-LAIN. Christ-cross-line; the alphabet formerly so called.

CRISTEN. A small kind of plum.

CRITCH. A bulging pitcher or big pan, as a butter critch.

CROCK. A bulging iron pot.

CROOPY. To sink one's body, bending down the thighs behind the legs.

CROWD. An apple pie, or apple cake; a fiddle.

CROWSHELL. The fresh water mussel shell (*unio*). The *uniones* are thus called because the crows take them from the water and open them, and, having eaten their bodies, leave them in the meadows.

CROWGARLICK. Allium vineale.

CRUDS. Curds

CRUMP UP. Bend or fold up, as if for warmth under excessive cold.

CRUMPLEN. A small apple, crumpled from bad or constrained growth.

CROUSTY. Crusty; ill-humoured.

CRUNDELS. The glands of the neck. Kernels.

CUBBY-HOLE. A snug place for a child, as between his father's knees.

CUE. The shoe of an ox.

CULVER. (A.S. culfre.) The wood pigeon, or ring dove.

CUNNEN MAN. A cunning man, or wizard; a low kind of seer.

CURDLE. Curl.

CUT. A mowing crop, as of grass. "A good cut of hay this year."

CUT, CUTTY, CUTTY WREN. The kitty wren (*troglodytes vulgaris*.)

CWOFFER. A coffer, chest.

D

DABSTER. One skilful in a game or art.

DADDER, Dather, or Dudder. To confound; to bewilder, or entangle. (A.S. *dyderian*.) "Me thinceth thæt thu me dwelige and dyderie." "Methinks thou deceivest and bewilderest me."—*Boet*. 35, 5.

DAFFIDOWNDILLY. Daffodil (*narcissus*).

DAG. A small stump of a branch.

DAG, or Chilldag. A chilblain.

DAKE. To prick or run in a point.

DAKER. A whetstone; dakerpouch. (*See* Budget.)

DALL IT. Confound it. Dall is most likely a mild substitute for a naughty word.

DANGEROUS. In danger, as will as dangerous to another.

DANK. Damp.

DAP. To bound as a ball.

DAPS. A likeness as if a cast from the same mould. "He's the very daps of his father."

DARK. Blind. "She's quite dark."

DAWDLEN. Slow and inefficient in work. Dawdling.

DEAD-ALIVE. Dull; inactive; moping.

DE-DA. Simple; foolish; of inactive mind and body.

DENT. A dint; a hollow mark made by a blow. "He beleeved his fingers made a dint upon her flesh."—*Ovid's Metamorph.*

DEWBERRY. A large kind of blackberry.

DEWBIT. The first meal in the morning, not so substantial as a regular breakfast. The agricultural labourers, in some parts of Dorsetshire, were accustomed some years since to say, that in harvest time they required seven meals in the day: dewbit, breakfast, nuncheon, cruncheon, nammit, crammit, and supper. But this seems to have been rather a quaint jingle than an enumeration of meals, as some of them, nuncheon and nammit, for example, clearly indicate the same.

DIBS. A children's game of toss and catch, played mostly by two with five dibs or knuckle-bones of a leg of mutton or round pieces of tile or slate.

DIDDEN. Did not.

DIEDAPPER. Divedapper. The dabchick.

DILL-CUP (E.) A buttercup.

DISFUGURE. To disfigure.

DISHWASHER. The water wagtail.

DITTER, or Datter, or Tig. A game of touch and run among children.

DOB. A dab; a knob or lump, as of earth.

DOCK-SPITTER. A tool for pulling or cutting up of docks.

Dogs. And-irons.

Dore, as in dumbledore.

Dore (A.S.) A drone.

Dor (Frs.) Dull, foolish. "That were dum and dor." "That became dum and dull or foolish." *Oera Linda Book.* Thence Dormouse.

Doughbeaked. Of weak or inactive mind; half-witted.

Doust. Dust; chaff, used as stuffing for beds.

Dout. To put out; to extinguish.

Dowse. A dash, a blow.

Downdaishous. Audacious.

Downvall. A fall as of rain or snow. "We shall have a downvall avore night."

Drabble-tail. Having one's gown-tail dirty.

Drail of a plough. A toothed iron, projecting from the beam of a plough for hitching the horses to.

Drail. To draggle.

Drap. A drop. To drop. "I'll drap it into you" is a mild way of saying "I'll give you a good beating."

Drapes. Trapes.

Drash. To thresh.

Drashel (A.S). A flail. Also, a threshold. [This word affords one of many cases in which the folk—speech is full and distinctive, while English is defective. The *drashel*, in English the *flail*, consists of two staves; the *handstaff*, and the *vlâil*,—*flail* or *flegel*, flying staff, from the Angol-Saxon, *fleogan*, to fly,—connected with the handstaff by a free socket called a *runnen keaple*; a *capel* from the Anglo-Saxon *Ceafe*, a beak or nozzle: so that the flail is only one part of the tool, for which the English has no name.]

Dra't Fakkets. Draught, faggots. Faggots of long underwood.

Dra'ts. Shafts of a cart, &c.

Draty. Draughty: Full of draughts of air; as a cold house.

Drawlatchet. Walking lazily and slowly.

Drean. To drawl in speaking.

Dred the wold woman's needdle. Thread the old woman's needle; a game in which the children join hands, and the last leads the train under the lifted arms of the first two.

Dredgel (E.) A flail.

DREVE. To drive. To drëve a common, was to drive together all the stock on it, and pound such as were not owned by those who had a right of common. The hayward did so occasionally.

DRIBBLE. To shoot the taw weakly, and by small shots, towards the pound or a marble.

DRINGE, or Drunge. To dring.

DRING (S.), Drunge (N.) To throng, to press or push. "As soon as Joe got on his back he would dring en up ageän the wall," spoken of a horse.

DRIPPER. A small shallow tub to catch drippings or take slops.

DRISK. A fine small wind-driven mist.

DRITH, or Drowth. Thirst or drought.

DRONG, or Drongway. A narrow way between two hedges or walls.

DROSTLE. To thrust, squeeze, or push about; as in getting through a crowd.

DROVE. A way between hedges, where cattle are driven to or from fields. A narrow drove is a drong.

DROU. A narrow opening in a stone wall instead of a stile. (Portland.)

DROW. To throw.

DRUG. A drag for a wheel.

DRUSH. A thrush.

DRUB. To throb or beat. "My head do drub:" "My head throbs."

DUBBED, or Dubby. Blunt.

DUCKY STWONE. A Portland man wandering along the beech (after a ground sea) in search of hidden treasure discovered two of what the Portlander calls 'Ducky stones', or two lumps of silver weighing 6lb." (From a newspaper.)

DUCK, Duckish. The twilight, "In the duck of the even'en."

DUDDLES. Little dods or dumps. Thicky duddle. A food of flour and water boiled up.

DUMPY-TOPPED, Dubby-topped. As a knife with a rounded or blunt-pointed top.

DUMMET. The dusk.

DUMBLEDORE. The humblebee.

DUMPY. Short and thick, thence dumpling, a little dump.

DUNDUCKY. Of dun or dull hue; colourless.

DUNCH. Deafish, dull; "He's quite dunch."

DUNCHNETTLE. The dead nettle (*Lamium.*)

DUNCH-PUDDEN. Hard or plain pudding of only flour or water, without plums or suet.

DUNGY. Downcast, dull; as spoken of a horse, whence 'donkey.'

DUNNICK. A hedge sparrow.

DUN-PIDDLE. The kite, or moor buzzard.

DURNS. The upright posts of a door.

E.

'E. He.

EACOR. An acorn.

EACER. An acre.

EALE. Ale.

EARN. Earn.

EARNEST. Earnest.

EASEMENT. An easing as from pain.

EES. Yes.

EESTERDAY. Yesterday.

EET. Yet.

EE-GRASS. Aftermath. (A.S. Ed-gærs, Edise.)

EGER, Eiger. Sharp, sour as cider.

ELEMEN. Made of elm.

ELT. A young sow or pig.

ELTROT, Eltroot. The cow parsley (*anthrescus sylvestris.*)

EM. Them.

EMMET-BUT, or Emmet-hill. An ant-hill.

EMPT. To empty.

EN. Him.

ER. He.

ERISHING (W.) A second, not first, gleaning.

ETH. Earth.

EVE. To become damp, as a stone from condensation of vapour on its surface. "We shall hä râin; the stwones do eve."

EVET. An eft, an ewt. The Saxon is *Efete*, nearest to which is the Dorset *Evet*, and then the English *Eft*; but *Newt* seems to be a blunder of taking *an-ewt* for *a-newt*, and putting the *n* of the article on to the name. The sister Teutonic tongues show no such shape. *Ewt* may be a shortening of *Ewet*.

EVERY, OR Ever-grass. A species of grass; rye grass *(lolium perenne.)*

EVEMEN. Evening.

EX. An axle or axis.

EXE (A.S. eax.) An axle or axis. "Hwerfep on pære ilcan *eaxe*." "Turns on the same axis."—*Boeth.* xxviii."

F.

FADDLE. A Fardel; a pack or bundle.

FALL. The fall of the leaf; the autumn.

FALTER. To fail; as a crop. "I be a-afeard the teäties wull *falter*."

FANTOD. A fuss, fidget. "She's always in a fantod about Meäry."

FAY. To fit; to succeed; to answer; or go on favourably.

FEAST. A village wake.

FEASEN. Faces.

FESS. Fussy, meddling, and eager in what is going on. "There's a fess feller."

FIGGED-PUDDEN. Plum-pudding.

FINEG. Finnég; Not to answer the calls of duty. As not to play to trumps, as one ought, at cards. "You finëged." (*See* Fùrnèg.)

FLANNEN. Flannel.

FLICK or Flip. To snap lighly with a whip. To hurry, flit.

FLINDERS. Flying bits, as of a thing smashed.

FLING. To kick. Spoken of a horse.

FLIP. Very kindly or friendly in talking. "How flip 'e wer."

FLISKY. Flying, as mist.

FLOOK, or Fluke. A flat worm (*distoma hepatica*) found in the livers of coathed sheep, the plaice.

FLOP. A mass of thin mud.

FLOUNCE. A flinging or flying as of splashed water, or a falling into it.

FLOUSH. Flying, flouncing.

FLUMP. A heavy and flying fall.

FLUMMOCKS. To overcome; frighten; bewilder.

FLUSTER. A flying, hurriedly, about to do things as on a sudden call.

FLUSH. Fledged. Applying to birds; "The young birds be nearly flush."

FOB. The froth of the sea as it washes on the shore. (Portland.)

FOOCH. To push, poke.

FOOTY. Little; insignificant.

FOREFRIENDS (E.) Ancestors.

FORESHARE (Voresheäre.) The right to a parcel of the grass of a common meadow, for the "foreshare of the year, as from February to August, ere the common feeding by cattle."

FORESTERS (E.) Forestvlees. Horseflies.

FORRELS. The covers of a book.

FOUSTY. Fusty.

FOWGHT. Fought.

FRET (spoken of horses). A griping pain in the bowels when blown with too much fresh food.

FREEMARTEN. The female calf of a twin, of which the other is a bull.

FRITH, or VIRTH. Brushwood.

FROG-HOPPER. The whole of the genus *cicada* or *tettigonia* of Linnæus are often so called.

FUDDLED. Brothered, confused.

FURLEN, Furlong. A piece or strip of corn-ground, a furrow's length.

FURR. Foul or sticky matter, as that on a foul tongue in sickness.

FURMITY, Frumenty.

FURNIGG (W.) Forneg, as Fineg.

G.

GAD. A stake, or bar of metal.

GAFFLE. To dress or pad the less hardy parts of the body as for cudgel-playing.

GAKE, or Gawk. To go or stand and gape about idly.

GAKEY. One who gakes or gawks; a fool, a cookoo.

GALLY. To frighten, scare.

GALLY-BAGGER. A scare-beggar; a bugbear.

GALLY-CROW. A scarecrow.

Gammel (or Gambrel.) A bent staff, upon the two ends of which butchers hang carcases by the tendons of the hock.

Gammen. Play or sport with another.

Gannywedge. A thick wooden wedge, to open the split of thinner iron ones. (A.S.) Ganian, To yawn.

Gap. A large breach in a hedge, a small one being a shard.

Gapmouth (S.) The bird goatsucker or nightjar.

Gawk-hammer, Gake-hammer (N.) A silly gaping fellow (a gawky.) Fools formerly had sometimes for a bauble a blown bladder fastened to a stick for a handle. If it was ever called a gawk-hammer or a ninny-hammer; then the word applied to a silly man may mean having a head as empty as a fool's hammer.

Gawl. An opening, an empty place, a bare patch in growing corn. Sandgawl: A cleft or hollow as in chalk soil into which sand is washed.

Gawly. Having many gawls. Applied to land, spongy or wet.

Gay. Fresh or green. Applied to mown grass: "That's too gay to carry yet."

Gear. Tackle. Iregear, iron utensils; cidergear, cider-making apparatus.

Geate. A gate.

Gee, Jee. To fit; to work or go on well. "He an' I dön't gee."

Gee Ho. Go ho! Addressed to horses.

Giddygander. The early purple orchis *(orchis mascula,)* and the green-winged meadow orchis *(orchis morio)*, and other common species of orchis, are so called in the Vale of Blackmore.

Gi'e. To give; to yield. "The vrost do gi'e;" "The frost yields, or thaws."

Gi'e in. To give in; to give up a contest.

Gi'e out. To give out; to give up a pursuit; to cease, from inability to hold on any longer; to fail, especially as a weak part. "My lags do gi'e out."

Gifts. White spots on the finger-nails, believed to betoken coming presents. Of this it is a saying,

"Gifts on the thumb, sure to come;
Gifts on the vinger, sure to linger."

Gil'cup, or Giltycup. Giltcup; the buttercup, *(ranunculus bulbosus)*; so called from the gold-like gloss of its petals.

GILP. To boast.

GILTYCUP (S.E.) The buttercup.

GIMMY. A hinge of two parts, working on a joint.

GIRT. Great.

GLEAN. Glëne; to sneer; to smile jeeringly, or sneeringly.

GLEARE. To glaze as tiles or bricks.

GLIBBY (E.) Glidesome. Easy to swallow.

GLOW, Glaw, Glawoo. To stare; to watch with fixed and wide open eyes.

GLUTCH. To swallow; to glut; to gulp.

GNANG. (*See* Nang.)

GOD-LMIGHTY'S Cow, or, sometimes, the Lady-bird. The *cocinella septem-punctata*. Children will often catch this insect, and, as Howitt says children do in Germany, put it on the tip of a finger, repeating

> "Laidy bird! laidy bird! vlee away hwome;
> Your house is a-vire, your childern wul burn."

GOLLIKINS. By gollikins; an exclamation.

GOND, or Gund. A disease of sheep; a kind of itch spreading on the skin in yellow spots.

Goo by. Go by. Live or behave by. "Zome can preach well but don't goo by it."

GOO-CART. A wooden frame on truckles to shut a child in when he begins to walk.

Goo. "All the goo;" "All the fashion."

Goocoo. The cuckoo.

GOOCOO FLOWER. *The cardamine pratensis*, on which goocoo-spettle is often found.

GOOCOO SPETTLE. The frothy nidus of the *cicado spumaria*, attributed to the spitting of the cuckoo.

Goo wi', or goo after. To court; to go with, as a young man walks with his sweetheart. "He do goo wi' Polly Hine."

GOODHUSSY, Good-housewi'e (good housewife.) A thread-case, in which a good housewife kept her thread.

GOOD-NOW. Good neighbour; my good fellow; ironically, "You won't frighten me, good-now."

GOOGARY. Giddy; shaky.

GOOLD. Gold.

GOOLDEN-CHAIN. Laburnum.

GOOLDEN-DROP. A variety of wheat.

GOSSIP is still used about Wimborne for a godfather, or godmother. Godcib (gossip) in A.S. meant a good kinsman, or kinswoman, and in lower meaning a good friend, but we now use Gossip for the talk of the good friends, instead of themselves.

GOUT. An underground gutter.

GRAB. To snatch up greedily; akin to grapple, grasp, gripe, grip, &c. Also the crab-apple.

GRABBLE. To grab much and slightly. "There, mother, I drapped my apples an' Jack grabbled em all up."

GRABSTOCK. A young crab-tree, or the cutting of one.

GRAMF'ER. Grandfather.

GRAMM'ER. Grandmother.

GREISTEN, Gristen. Corn for grinding or ground.

GRETE. Very friendly; "How grete they two be."

GREYGLE. The *hyacinthus non scriptus.*

GRIBBLE. A young crab-tree or black-thorn; or a knotty walking stick made of it.

GRIDDLE. To grind corn very coarsely or imperfectly.

GRINTERN (S.) A compartment of a granary for threshed corn. *Ern* means a stead or place for a thing, so *grintern* may be a grindern for grindcorn—corn ready for grinding.

GRIP. A handful of wheat. Wheat is said to be in grip (handful) as it is left by the reapers.

GRIP, Grippy (E). To tie grips up into sheaves.

GROTTEN. A sheep-slade; a run or pasture for sheep.

GROUN'. A field. "Pleased down to groun'" is a hyperbole, meaning "pleased to the very toes."

GROUN'. "To groun' a pick" is to put the end of its stem on the ground, as a bearing in raising a pitch of hay.

GROUN' ASH. An ashen stick growing from the ground, and much tougher than a branch of the tree.

GROUT (W.) To grub or dig out a small ditch.

GUDGEN. A cutting of thorn or other wood driven into the ground to strike root.

GUDGEON (E). A short forked stake, used in hedging to fasten down a plusher or plesher.

GULDER. An intermediate or subsidiary flow of the tide about four hours and a-half after highwater. (Weymouth.)

GUMMY (W.) Thick; clumsy; as a gummy ankle.

GUNDY. Having the gund.
GURGENS. Pollard; coarse flour.
GUSS. A girth.
GWAIN. Going.
GWAINS on. Goings on; doings or behaviour.

H.

HA'. Have or has.
HACK. A word of brickmaking.
HACKER. A broad hoe.
HACKER. To strike the teeth together in a shaking from cold or fear.
HACKLE. A bee-hackle; a sheaf of straw forming a cloak or roof over a beehive.
HAG-ROD, hag-rode, or hag-ridden. The nightmare attributed to the supernatural presence of a witch or *hag*, by whom one is *ridden* in sleep.
HAGGLER. One who buys up poultry to sell again.
HAIL. Hale; sound; strong.
HAILS, Hayels, Haws. The fruit of the hawthorn. Haege (Sax.) means a hedge. Losing the g it became haw, and hay. Hence hawthorn means the hedge thorn. Then its fruit was called haws from haegas as (Sax.) and Hailes, from haegelas (Sax.), little hawfruits.
HAIN, or Winterhâin. To lay up grass land, not to stock it. "The meâd wer winterhäined."
HALTERATH. A bridle-path; a road for one on horseback, but not for a carriage.
HAM, Hamel. An inclosure, also a home in names of places.
HAMCHAW. To hem and haw ere giving an answer.
HAME. Haulm; the hollow stalks of plants, as beänhame, peashame, teätyhame, &c.
HAMES. The pieces of wood put on a collar of a horse with staples to take the traces.
HANDY. Useful; also near. Ready and good for use.
HANDWRIST. Wrist meant anything that wrings or writhes round as a swivel. Dorset kept the word hand, which was meant to show what wrist or wrest it was, for the neck and foot have wrists of some swivelish turning.
HANGEN. The sloping side of a hill.

HANGEN-HOUSE. A shed under a continuation of the roof of a house.

HANG-GALLIS. Hang-gallows; fit for the gallows; that ought to be, or is likely to be, hanged. "A hand-gallis rogue."

HAN'PAT: Fit or ready at hand: at one's fingers' ends. "He had it all han'pat."

HAN'SEL. A hand gift. Something given to a young woman at her wedding towards housekeeping is called a good "han'sel" in the Vale of Blackmore.

HAPS. A hasp.

HAPPER. To hop much or patter; as falling hail.

HARD. A hard boy, is a big boy; hard being opposed to tender, in a child of tender years.

HARDLE. To entangle. (*See* Tardle).

HARD-WORKEN. Industrious.

HARROW of a gate. The backer upright timber of a gate by which it is hung to its post. The one in the middle, between the harrow and the head, is the midde spear, which is also the name of the upright beam that takes the two leaves of a barn's door.

HARUM-SCARUM.

HARNESS. Tackle; as cider harness, for making cider.

HARREL (E.) To harl (*see* Hardle). Tangle.

HART-BERRY. The whortle-berry; bilberry (*vaccinium*.)

HARVEST-MAN. The cranefly, or daddy-long-lags (*tipula oleracea*).

HA'SKIM-CHEESE. Halfskim cheese; cheese made of milk skimmed only once.

HASKETS (E.) Hazel and maple bushes. Brushwood.

HASSEN. Hast not.

HASSOCK, Hassick. A tuft of sedge or brushwood.

HATCH. A wicket or little low garden-gate; a half-door. (A.S. hæca.)

HATCH (W.) Hitch.

HATCHES (W.) Double gates, as to a farm yard.

HAVE. To have something done is much used for to cause it to be done, as "I'll have the pony a-clipped." "I'll have a cowhouse a-builded." "I'll have the child a-brought hwome."

HAVES, Heps. The fruit of the wild rose. Johnson calls heps or hips the fruit of the hawthorn. I think not; they are haïels (N.) or haws.

Hâv. The spikelet of the oat. "The woats be out in hâv."

Haw, Hawoo. Ahoe.

Hawked, or howked cow. A cow with a white or white-patched face.

Hawledge. The work or cost of hawling.

Haymaiden. A plant of the mint tribe; ground ivy (*glechoma hederacea*.) Used for making a medicinal liquor, "häymaïden tea."

Haymeaken. Haymaking formerly consisted of several operations which, with fine weather, commonly followed each other in Dorsetshire thus: The mown grass—in zwath, swath—was thrown abroad—tedded—and afterwards turned once or twice; in the evening it was raked up into little ridges—rollers—single or double, as they might be formed by one raker, or by two raking against each other; and sometimes put up into small cones or heaps, called cocks. On the following morning the rollers or cocks were thrown abroad in passels (parcels), which, after been turned, were in the evening put up into large ridges—weäles; and the wales were sometimes pooked, put up into larger cones—pooks—in which the hay was loaded. In raking grass into double rollers, or pushing hay up into wales, the fore raker or pickman is said to rake in or push in, or row or roo, and the other to close.

Hayward. A warden of the fences or of a common, whose duty it was to see that it was not stocked by those who had no right of common. He sometimes "drove the common"—*i.e.*, drove all the stock in it into a corner, and pounded such as was not owned by those who had a right of common.

Hazen. In some parts the same as hiëssen; to forebode.

Head. "To zet ther heads together." To consult or conspire. The word conspire is itself from *con*, together, and *spiro*, to breathe, which conspirators do while "setting their heads together." Thence the Persians call an intimate friend *humdum*, from *hum*, together, and *dum*, breath.

Headland, or Hedlèn. The ground or ridge under hedge, at the heads of the ridge where the horses turn in ploughing.

Heal. To cover; hide. "To hëal bëans." "To earth up beans." "The house is unhëaled." "The house is stripped," as by a rough wind.

Healen, Hellen. Stones; flag-stones for roofing, whence hellier a roofer.

Hean. The handle, as of a knife. "The knife's a-broke off up to the heän."

HEARE NUT. *Bunium Flexuosum.* Hares are fond of its green leaves. Boys eat its roots or nuts in the spring.

HECKLE-O'-VAN. A kind of hackle or little hut, as of grass or straw, in which to sit hidden so as to shoot birds that come nigh. (Heard once in Dorset. Is it a Dorset word?)

HEDLEN. Headlong; giddy; precipitate. "There's a hedlèn chile."

HEELTAPS, Heletaps. When the beer or ale of a barrel has been drawn off down to the lowest tap, that which is left below it cannot flow out but by the heeling or hanging over of the barrel, and is called the heeltap. "As the liquor of a heeled tap or cask." To heel, to hang or lean over is used in seamanship, as "The ship heels," and in Dorset "Shall I hële ye out a glass o' eäle." The word hele means to pour out. It first meant to hele or heel the jug. In the Isle of Wight heeltaps is used for liquor left at the bottom of a drinker's glass, and it may be said to him "Take off your heeltaps," or clear your glass. Heeltaps from the dregs, if even free from dregs, are not at all highly rated and to call beer heeltaps is to give it a bad name.

HEFT. Weight.

HELE. To pour out fluid. "Shall I hële out another cup?"

HELRUT (Portland). The herb Alexanders. *Smyrnium Olusatrum.* Is the name healroot? Turner, A.D. 1548, gives it as kept by "Poticaries."

HEMP (Spinning). Some words used in spinning of hemp are, I believe, Swift—the spinning wheel. Fleäre—outsticking onhanging fibres of hemp on newly spun twine. Skimps—bits of hemp rind or the like hanging on newly spun twine.

HERENCE. Hence.

HERERIGHT. Here on the spot; at once.

HET. Heat. An American who came hither from Dorchester, in America, the daughter town of our Dorchester, was heard to call "heat" "het."

HETH. The hearth, or a heath.

HETHCROPPER. A pony bred on a heath.

HIC A'TER HOCK, or Hicker to hacker. The pursued seemingly pursuing the pursuer. If a dog were running round in a broad ring after a hare, and the hare were farther than half of the ring before the dog, he would seem to be the catcher. A man, telling of seeing such a case of hounds and hare, said "There they went hicker to hacker all auver, John's hounds avore and the heare a'ter.

HICK. To hop on one leg.

HIDE. To whip.

HIDY-BUCK. The game of hide and seek.

HIESSEN. To forebode evil. "'T'll ráin avore night," says one. "There don't be hiëssenny," answers another, who hopes it may not.

HIGH. "Why don't ye come to church, John?" "O, Mr. H. is too high vor me." This does not mean that his teaching was too high, but that his sermons were high in hard words of Latin and Greek, so that he could not understand them.

HIGHLOWS. A kind of high shoes, lower than kitty boots.

HIKE OFF, or out. To go off hastily by compulsion, or actively to expel. "You shall hike out."

HILE. Ten sheaves of corn set up in the field, four on each side and one at each end, and forming a kind of roof. So a N. C. word for a hile is huttock, a little hood or stook; and two sheaves put on the top of the stock are called hood-sheaves or hoods.

HIPE. A heap.

HIPPITY-HOPPITY. Hoppingly.

HITCH. To hang up or on. "Hitch in the horses." "They wer a-hitched up." "They were arm-in-arm."

HITH, Heith. Height.

HIZZUF, Hisself. Himself.

HO. Anxious care. "I don't know and don't ho." "He ymbe manegra theóda thearfe hogode." He was careful for many nations.—"Ælfric's Homily on St. Gregory.

HOBBLE. A kind of open field-shed for cattle to go under in bad weather.

HOBBLE. To tie an animal's legs to keep him from wandering.

HOBBLE. A coarsely loud laugh.

HOBBLES. A wooden instrument to confine the legs of a horse while he is undergoing an operation.

HOBBLY-HOY, or Hobbledy-hoy. Define by a rhyme—"Neither man nar boy."

HOG. A sheep one year old.

HOILS. The beard or awn of barley.

HOLD wi'. To hold or side with; to follow in opinion. "To hold wi' the häire, an' run wi' the houns."

HOLLABALOO. A noisy uproar.

HOLM, Höm. Holly, especially low and more prickly holly.

HOLROD. The Cowslip (Swanage). Is it the same as the Helrut of Portland?

HOMBLE. A duck.

HOME SCREECH (W.) The missel thrush.

HOMMICKS. Clumsy boots.

HONEY-ZUCK. The honeysuckle.

HOOK (Somerset, hoke.) To gore with the horns. "A hookèn bull." "A bull that gores."

HOOP. The bulfinch.

HOP. So used for to crack by heat. "I've a-hoppt my bwiler."

HOPSCOTCH. A game of children, consisting of hopping over a parallelogram of scotches or chalk lines on the ground."

HORNET (E). The common wasp.

HORRIDGE, Whorage. A house or nest of bad characters.

HO'S ADDER (W.C.) The dragon fly.

Hoss, Ho's. A horse. Also, a plank or faggot to stand upon when digging in wet ditches, moved forwards by a knobbed stick put through it. "Not to hitch oon's hosses together." "Not to agree or coincide in opinion." The shaft-horse or wheel-horse of a team is called a thiller, from the A.S. thill, a shaft or pole; the next before him the body-hoss, being by the waggoner's body. The next forward is the lash-horse, being within reach of his lash while keeping by the side of the body-horse; and the fourth would be a vollier, or fore-hoss.

HOSS-TINGER. The dragon-fly (*libellula.*)

HOSS-TONGUE. Hart's tongue (*scolopendrium vulgare.*)

HOUNCE. To hound or hunt out.

HOUNDS, or Bussels, of a waggon. The slides or fellow-pieces.

HOUNTISH. Doggish, snappish, snarling.

HOWSH. A cry to swine, to stir them onwards.

HUCKLE. The hip.

HUCKMUCK. Dirty, slovenly.

HUCKMUCK. A wicker strainer put in a mashing tub to keep the grain from coming out with the wort.

HUD (from hood.) The hull or legume of a plant.

HUDDICK, Huddock. (N.C. hottle; Norfolk and Suffolk, hutkin; all diminutives of hood.) A bag or case for a sore finger. In the northern counties the covered cabin of a coal-barge is a huddock.

HUMBUZ. A thin piece of wood with a notched edge; which, when swung round swiftly on a string, yields a humming or buzzing sound.

HUMMICK. A heat or sweat.

HUMSTRUM. A rude musical instrument.

HUNGERED. Hungry. An hungered. (Matt. xii. 1. and elsewhere.)

HURDLEVOOT. A wryfoot, not a clubfoot.

HUSTLE (E.) To moan, spoken of the wind.

HUZ-BIRD, Whore's-bird. Bird meaning child, a naughty name by which anger sometimes calls a child. It does not seem that the becaller, sometimes a mother! always knows the meaning of it.

HWOME. Home to the place at which a body is fastened, as a knife to its handle or an arm to the shoulder; "Broke the zive huome to the sneäd."

HYTHE. A landing stead or haven. This old Saxon word is yet living among us by Portland, for the hythes at which the fish are landed on the coast that borders on the Fleet, as Chickerell hythe, Langton hythe, &c. It is the name of Hythe in Kent.

I.

ICE-CANDLE. An icicle.

IF so be. This old English wording, as often heard in Dorset. (II. Corinthians v. 3.)

ILES (W.) The same as ayels (N.) The awns as of barley.

IMMA'BBEE. It may be.

INJIST. Almost; very nearly.

INON. An onion.

INON-RWOPE. An onion rope; a rope or string of onions.

IRE-GEAR. Iron ware.

J.

JA, Jaw. A tenon for a mortise.

JACK-IN-THE-GREEN. The polyanthus.

JACK-RAG. "Every jack-rag ö'm" means every single individual.

JACK-O-LENT, a Jack-of-Lent. A scarecrow of old clothes, sometimes stuffed. The name is taken from that of a ragged and lean figure formerly shown in some Lent procession, and betokening the Lent fast.

JAMS. Wire shirt-buttons, of which many used to be made at and near Blandford.

JANDERS. The jaundice.

JEEMINEI, or Good Jeeminei (N.) A cry of wonder; at something that another puts forth. Oh! brave!

JIB (W.) A handbarrow, as a pig-jib for pig killing.

JIMMY. The hinge of a door.

JIST, Jis'. Just; jist about.

JIT (S.E.) To jog, to jut.

JOBBLER. Underground jobbler: the bird wheatear.

JONNICK. Jolly (Purbeck.)

JONNICK (W., N., S.E.) Honest, fair, straightforward. "Come, play jonnick: noo shufflèn."

JOPPETY-JOPPETY. To express the nervous trepidation caused by being flurried or much rated—"an' there I wer all joppety-joppety." I believe it means the feeling as if the whole body were jumping with the strong beating of the heart, for I suppose jop means a little jump, and jopp'et a very small or quick one.

JUT. To give one a sudden blow or nudge when still, particularly when writing. "Don't jut zoo." "She jutted 'en." "She nudged him."

K.

KEAF (W.) Waste of short straws, &c., in threshing. This is just the Saxon ceaf, chaff.

KEAFEN REAKE. A rake to clear the ceaf, from the corn.

KEEP. Food for cattle—"We've hardly keep enough."

KILLICK STWONE (E.) A stone used by fishermen as an anchor when fishing for pout, conner, &c.

KILLICK RWOPE (E.) The rope that fastens the killick stone to the boat.

KNACKER. A knacker is defined in the earlier share of the Dorset Glossary as a buyer of old out-worn horses for dogs' meat. Bailey gives a knacker as a collar-maker for horses, and the word is now used for a harness-maker in Norfolk, and, it may be, elsewhere, and nothing is more likely than that a harness-maker should have taken such an agency from horse owners, their customers. "Knacker's-hole, near Ockford Fitzpaine, might have been a lonesome spot fit for the knacker's work of the putting of a poor old horse for ever out of harness.

KECKS, or Kex. A stock of hemlock or cow parsley.

KEE (W.) To tire out.

KEEPEN. Keeping of a song; the burden or refrain of a song.

KEEVE or Kive. A large tub used for the wort to work in when brewing. (A.S. cyf a vat.)

KEECH. To cut grass and weeds in water.

KEECHING-ZIVE. A scythe for keeching.

KERF. The cut of a saw in wood.

KERNEL. This word is commonly applied to the pips of pomaceous fruit, which are sometimes playfully shot from between the thumb and forefinger by young folks after saying

"Kernel, come, kernel! hop over my thumb,
And tell me which way my true-love will come;
East, west, north, or south,
Kernel, jump into my true-love's mouth."

KERP (W.) To crip; to talk mincingly.

KETCH. To set or harden, as melted fat.

KETCHER. The membrane over the viscera of a pig.

KEYS. The seed vessels of the sycamore and maple.

KEAKEHARN. The windpipe, particularly of a slaughtered animal.

KEAPLE. The running socket in which a flail was fastened to the handstaff.

KID. A pod or legume, as a beän-kid, a pea-kid.

KIND. Sleek, as spoken of fur; also keen as of a knife.

KIT. All the whole kit o'm;" "All the whole set, or tribe, of kindred."

KITPAT or Kitbat. The clogged grease in the stocks of wheels.

KITTICO. To push with one's elbows, as in getting through a crowd.

KITTYBOOTS. A kind of short laced boots, reaching up only over the ancles.

KITTY-COOT. The water-rail.

KIVE. (See Keeve.)

KLINK OFF. To go off as closely or unobserved as may be.

KNAP. The yet unopened flower head of the potato and some other plants. "The teäties be out in knap." A small hillock or rising, what is called in Somerset "a batch;" the brow of a hill. (A.S. cnaep).

KNEE-KNAPS. Leathers worn over the knees by thatchers at work.

KUVVEL. A tub with holed ears to take a stang wherewith to carry it.

L.

Lag. Leg.

Laggens. Leggings; short gaiters.

Lagwood. The bigger loppings of a tree.

Laiter. One laying of eggs ere a hen's sitting.

Lam's Grass. Spring grass; early grass; as distinguished from eegrass.

Laminger. One become lame.

Lamploo. An outdoor game amongst boys.

Larrence, Lawrence. From some cause, which the author has not yet found, Lawrence is in some parts of Dorset the patron or personification of laziness. When one is seen to be lazy Lawrence is said to have him, and when one feels a loathing of work he sometimes cries

"Leäzy Larrence, let me goo!
Don't hold me zummer an' winter too."

Lark's Lease. The Cowlease is bounded to the cows by fences, but since fences are nothing to larks a lark's leäse is unbounded. "The business is all at lark's lease" means it is not brought within any lines within which it can be settled.

Lathy. Tall and thin.

Latten. Tin. It is glossed in English as a kind of brass, or rather tin plate, as distinguished from the metal tin.

Lauten-yeat (W.) A great hurry.

Lavish. Rank. "That wheat is lavish."

Lawk. Look! Behold! A word of surprise among women.

Lawn, or **Lawnd.** Unploughed land; the unploughed part of an arable field.

Lawn (W.) A natural terrace, such as is often seen on the sides of the hills and downs; a linch or linchet.

Lawnder. An iron in the forepart of a sull, sliding on the lawn, or lawnd, before it is turned.

Leade. To dip up or draw off a liquid. [A.S. hladan. 'hládath nú:'] 'Draw out now.'—*John* ii. 8.

Leades. Raves of a waggon.

Leadecart. A cart with raves, so as to be loaded with hay or straw.

Leady's Cushin. The thrift, *Amieria vulgaris* (Portland.)

Lear. An ailing in sheep.

Lease. To glean after the reapers. (A.S. Lesan, to gather.)

LEASE-CARN. Corn gleaned.

LEAT. To leak.

LEAVE. To lade out a liquid.

LEAZE, or Zummerleäze. A field stocked through the summer, in distinction from a mead which is mown; thence ewsleäse, cowleäse. [A.S.]—Læsu-pasture. "Ic drife mine sceáp to heora læse." "I drive my sheep to their lease."—*Ælfric's Dialogue.*

LEDGERS. Rods that are fastened down by spars on the thatch of a rick or house.

LEER, or Leery, or Larry (W.) Empty in the stomach; wanting food. "Weary and Leary;" or as a leer, empty waggon.

LENCE. The loan of any thing. "I thank ye-var the lence ö't."

LENTCROCK. Crockery sherds, formerly thrown and smashed by boys on Shrove Tuesday.

LE's, Let's. Let us.

LET. A stooping or interruption; used by boys playing marbles. "Let shall be." "An accidental stopping shall be fair."

LEVERS or Livers, Lëver or Liver-leaves. The great yellow flag or its leaves.

LEW. Screened from the wind; lee. Shelter from the wind. "In the lew zide, o' the hedge." [A.S. hleow, or hleo, shelter, warmth.]

LEW; lew-warm. Luke-warm.

LEWTH. Shelter from the wind. [A.S. on thesses holtes hleo."] "In this holt's shelters." Warmth "Come to the lew o' the vire."

LIBBETS. Rags in strips.

LIE. The lie of the country; the relative position of places. I thought I coodden be wrong, by the lie of the country.

LIE-BOX. A box for making lie from wood-ashes.

LIEF. "Lief," as willingly, or soon. This old English word was heard in Dorset by a friend in 1875.

LIGGET. Small bit, or rag. "Every ligget o't."

LIGHT, or Light-headed. Delirious.

LIKE, in Dorset, as in some other counties, qualifies an adjective. "He's down-hearted like:" "He is rather down-hearted." "He is all muopèn like."

LIKE. The Hindoostani *sa, se, si,* is so used as "Ek kala sa g'hora. "A black-like horse."

LIMBER. Very limp; flaccid.

LIMBERS. The shafts of a waggon.

LIMBLESS. "I'll knock thee limbless:" "I'll knock thee to pieces; thy limbs off."

LIMMER. A painter, an artist.

LINCEN. Lincen. An intensitive of size; as "a lincèn girt heäre."

LINCHET or Linch. A ledge of ground on the side of a hill; or the strip of green ground between two ledges. [A.S. hlinc.]

LINDED. A linded cow; a cow with a white streak down her back.

LINE. To lean.

LINHAY, Linnedge. A low-roofed shed attached to a house; a penthouse.

LINNET. Lint; tinder.

LIN-MAN. A man in the flax-trade.

LIP. A vessel; a seed-lip, or seed-box, in which a sower carried his seed. [A.S. leap.]

LIPPEN, or Lippy. Wet, rainy. "'Tis a very lippy time." "The weather is very rainy, or stormy."

LISSEN. A streak or layer; a stratum. "There's a lissen o' bad hay in thik rick."

LITSOME, or Lissom. Lithesome; of light and cheerful mind.

LITTEN (W.) A long tale. A long noise.

LITTER. A lot of loose things lying about.

LITTY. Of light and easy bodily motion.

LIVERS. Same as Levers.

LOGGY (S.E.) To lag, loiter much. To play truant from school. "I never logged vrom school."

LO'K ZEE. Look, see you.

LONG. "By long an' by leäte"; after a long time, and much ado.

LOOK SHARP. To be quick; to make haste.

LOP, Loppy. To lounge about lazily and idly. "Don't loppy about here: goo an' do zome'at."

LOPLOLLY. One who lops and lolls; a lazy or idle person.

LOT, or 'low. To allot or allow; to think or suppose. "'E do wish hizzuf out o't, I do 'lot, or "I do 'low."

LOTE, or lo't; also lart. A loft; the floor of an upper room; the ceiling. "I can reach up to the lote."

LOUP. A kind of sea louse, somewhat like a wood louse, which, in warm summer weather, eats the bait which fishermen set in lobster pots.

LOWSEN. To listen.

LUG. A pole. A pole in land measure is 5½ yards.

LUMPER. To stumble; to tread loosely.

LUMPY. Heavy.

LURE. A disease of sheep; an ulcer in the cleft of the foot.

LURRY. A litten.

LWOTH. Loath; unwilling.

M.

MADAM is used in Dorset instead of Mrs., as a mark of supérior respect to ladies. "Madam A gi'ed me thease frock."

MADDERS, or Mathers. The stinking chamomile *(anthemis cotula.)*

MADE STONE. Stone rough hewn at the Quarry. Make stone, to hew it.

MAG. A mark or stake to throw at, as in quoits or pitch-half-penny. Also the name of a game among boys, in which the players throw at a stone set up on edge.

MAGOT. A whim or fancy.

MAGOTY. Fanciful; fond of experiments; crotchety. "What a magoty man he is."

MAIDEN TREE. Not a pollard. It was believed that if a young maiden ash were split, and a ruptured child drawn through it, he would become healed. The author has known of two trees through which children have been so drawn. In addition to what I have already said of a maiden tree or maiden stick, I would quote the words of a friend:—"It is an axiom here that none but a plant raised from a seed and never cut off will produce decent timber The idea of maiden is no doubt this—that the plant has never produced anything by way of offspring; thus a polling, or any such cutting off, results in the production of several shoots or stems, and if one only of these be allowed to grow yet it never becomes good timber."—O.P.C.

MAIN. [A.S. mægen, might; used also as an adjective mighty.] "A main girt tree." "A mighty or very great tree." Comp. "With might and main."

MAINPIN of a waggon. A pin put through the fore-axle of a waggon for it to turn upon in locking.

MAINTAINANCE (W.) Manure spread over land.

MAMMET. An image; a scarecrow.

MAMPUS, mumpus. A great number; a crowd. "A mampus o' volk."

MANDY. Saucy.

MAN or Maun. [A.S. mand.] A maund; a large withy basket with two handles, for apples, potatoes, &c., of the shape of a frustrum of a cone. "Sweet smelling apples in a maunde, made flat of osier twigges.'—*Ovid's Metam.*

MANY. Used for much, as in Anglo-Saxon. "Do the cows gi'e many milk?" So "few" is used as a noun, as "We have a goodish 'few' of apples." The words *maenig* and *feo* were nouns in Saxon.

MARRELS, Merrels. The old game of "nine men's morris."

MARK VOR. To show tokens of becoming. "He do mark vor to be tall."

MARTEN. A heifer that does not breed. (*See* Freemarten).

MASH-MORTAR. "To beat all to mash-mortar."

MAWKEN. A kind of mop for the oven.

MAZZERDY. Knotty.

MEADEN. Same as madders.

MEAL OF MILK The milk of one milking.

MEARY'S TEARS. The Spotted liverwort. As a friend writes to me:—"At Osmington, and no doubt elsewhere in our county, there is a survival of a sweet, simple, old-world piece of folk-lore about the spotted liverwort. The cottagers like to have it in their gardens, and call it 'Mary's Tears.' The legend is that the spots on the leaves are the marks of the tears shed by St. Mary after the Crucifixion. Further, and this is to me a quite unknown tradition, her eyes were as blue as the fully opened flowers, and by weeping the eyelids become as red as the buds."—H.J.M.

MEASONER. A mason.

MEAT-WEARE. Food stuff.

MEECH, Mooch, Mouch. To gather up things by picking, or begging.

MEESH. Moss.

MEL. To meddle.

MENT. [A.S. myntan.] To resemble, as 'He do ment his brother.'

MERRY. The wild cherry.

MEESH. The run or lair of a hare.

METHER Ho! Come hither ho! A carter's call to a horse in driving.

MID. May, or might.

MIFF. A slight mind-chafing with coolness between friends.

MIGGY, Muggy. Misty, as weather.

MILLER, or Millard. A large white moth that flies at twilight, such as the puss-moth, or the pale tussock-moth. Children sometimes catch these moths, millers, and, having interrogated them on their taking of toll, make them plead guilty, and condemn them in these lines:—

"Millery, millery, dowsty poll,
How many zacks hast thee a-stole?
Vow'r an' twenty an' a peck,
Hang the miller up by's neck."

MIMPS (E.) To hesitate, coquet.

MIND. To put in mind as well as to bear in mind. "Mind me o't to morrow."

MIN. As much as to say, "You must know I bent afeared o' thee min."

MINNETS. In marble play, knuckle down. "Noo minnets," not clear away any little things from before the taw.

MINT. A mite.

MINTY. Having mints (mites) in it, as rotten cheese.

MIXEN. [A.S. mixen.]

MIZ. Mishappening. "This is a miz job."

MIZ-MARE. A mare.

MOCK. The stump of a wride as of hazel or other wood, or a tuft of sedge grass.

MOMMET (W.) A guy, an effigy.

MONEYSPIDER. The *aranea scenica*, which, when they see it hanging on its thread, folks sometimes take and try to swing it round their head three times without throwing it off; and then put it into their pockets whither it is believed it will soon bring money.

MOOT. The bottom of the stem of a felled tree, with its roots.

MOPE (W.) The bulfinch.

MORE. The tap-root of a plant.

MOTE. As a strawmote, a stem of grass.

MOUEL. A field mouse (*mus sylvaticus*).

MOULD. The top of the head or skull.

MOWBURNT (E). As corn or hay, burnt by heating in the mow or rick.

MOWBURN'D. Mowburnt.

MUCKLE (E). Furze or heath laid in on the top of a drain ere the earth is cast in.

MUCH. To smooth down; as a cat's hair.

MULLUM. Soft and crumbling: as a mullum cheese.

MUMMOCK. A fancy figure, an effigy, a guy.

MUMMERS. A set of youths who sometimes go round at Christmas tide, beprimed with ribbons and tinsel, with a fellow one for "Father Christmas" to act a little play of a fight between a Turkish knight and King George of England.

MUMP. One who is wont to beg of her neighbours.

MUMPUS. (*See* Mampus).

MUTTON-TOPS. Lamb's quarters. The young shoots of the Goosefoot (*chenopodium*), sometimes boiled as a food-wort.

MWOPE. The bullfinch.

MWORISH. So good as to give a wish to have more of it.

N.

NAISE. Noise. A scolding. "To drëve a nâise" is an expression which means to keep up or keep making a noise. So "Don't ye drëve sich work," means "Do not make such an uproar."

NAMMET. A.S. Non-mere, Noon meat. A luncheon. (*See* Dewbit.)

NANG or Nangy. To mock one by half-clear sounds wagging the jaw with a grin. A great insult "enough to meäke oone's blood bwile."

NAPS, Knee-naps. Leathers worn over the knees by thatchers at work.

NAR, Never. "Nar a cow." Never a cow.

NEAR. Stingy, miserly.

NEEDS (genitive of *need*.) Of necessity.

NESH. (A.S. Nesc. or hnesc.) Tender.
———— "the nesh tops
Of the young hazel."—*Crowa's Lewesdon Hill.*
"This meat is nësh." "Da veel nësh."

NESSELTRIPE. The most weakly or last of a brood of fowls, a fare of pigs, or a family of children.

NETLENS or Knotlens. The same as Chetlens.

NETTLE. To sting another's mind with words.

NEVER'S TIDE. A tide that never comes—like the Greek calends.

NEVER-THE-NEAR. Never the nigher; never the more for that.

NEWST (W.) Very nearly.

NEX'-KIN. Very like; very nearly so; next of kin. "If tidden robbèn oone, 'tis nex'-kin to it."

NIB. A rough timber carriage of two high wheels on a wooden axle and shafts, used for drawing of trees out of the wood.

NICKY. A very small short-cut bundle of wood for lighting fires.

NIGGLE, Naggle. To complain of trifles from ill temper or bad humour.

NINNYHAMMER. A silly body. (*See* Gawkhammer.)

NINNYWATCH, Nunnywatch. The following is a bit of talk about the word Ninnywatch between a worthy Dorset gentleman and two of his parish folks, J. and P. and M. M.: "There, sir; the p'liceman twold I zome'hat that put me in a terr'ble ninny-watch." "And what's that?" says I. "Well, sir, I d'low, 'tis trouble," quoth P. (Enter J.) "Did you ever hear of a ninny-watch?" J.: "O, ees, sir, I've often a-heärd em tell o't." "Well, what does it mean?" J.: "I d'low 'tänt got noo meänen, sir; 'tis only oone o' they words we poor folk do use." "Old P. tells me it means 'trouble.'" J.: "Trouble, sir; dwoant meän trouble noo mwore than do meän Richard." "Well, then, how do you use it?" J.: "Well, sir, if I've a-zeed anybody in ar-a-bit of a bumble about his work—a-peepèn about—in a kind of stud like—I've a-heard em say "What be you got a-ninny-watchèn about?" Ninnywatch is most likely a "ninny's outlook" as for he knows not what.

NIPPER, Knipper. A boy just about old enough to go out to work. Knip is, I suppose, the Saxon *cnapa*, a boy, and *er* makes it mean a biggish boy. "When I wer a nipper, vök diden do as they do now."

NIPPY. Quick-minded, sharp, alive to things of the minute.

NIPPY. Hungry, with a keen appetite. "I be rather nippy."

NIRRUP. A donkey.

NIT. Not yet.

NITCH. A burthen; as much as one can carry of wood, hay, or straw, and sometimes of drink. Hedgers are sometimes allowed to carry home every night a nitch of wood, which they put on the end of a pole called a *speäker*, spiker.

Nog (knog). A big knob, whence nogger, a very big knob. "A girt knog ô cheese." A nugget is a small knob.

Noggerhead. A loggerhead; a blockhead.

Noohow. After no regular mode or shape. "Theäse rick's a-meäde noohow."

Noowhen. At no time.

Not (A.S. hnot). Hornless, as a not cow; a not sheep.

Nother (A.S., Nather). Neither. "You can't do it." "Nor you nother." "Nother of flesh ne of blod."—*Lives of the Saints.*

Nudge. To jog one, as with the elbow.

Nunch, Nunchen. A lunch or luncheon.

Nu'ss. To nurse.

Nut. The stock of a wheel.

O.

O'. Of.

O' Zundays. On Sundays.

Oben. Open.

Odds. Difference. "What odds is that to you?"

Off. The line from which boys begin to shoot at marbles.

Off vor. How be off vor apples to year. "He's bad off."

O'n, O'en. For of him.

Onlight. To alight, get off horse.

Ooser, oose, or wu'se. A mask as with grim jaws, put on with a cow's skin to frighten folk. 'Wurse,' in Layamon's Brut, is a name of the arch-fiend.

Ope. An opening in the cliffs down to the water side (Portland).

Organy. A plant of the mint tribe. Marjoram or Pennyroyal, or both.

Orts. Leavings from hocks of hay with which cows are fed afield. "Can feed on orts," Ben Johnson in an ode.

O's. Of us.

Ounse. A ring as of wood or iron fastened as an eyelet in a noose at one end of a waggon rope to hold the running end. This word seems to be akin to *hounds* in shipping. Holes in the cheek of the mast wherein the ties run, '*Hound* and *hand*' both mean what takes or holds. Ounse might be Hounse.

Our. Is often put in Dorset before the name of a brother or sister, as our Jim or our Meäry.

OUT OV AXEN. Out of asking. Having had one's banns of marriage published three times.

OUTSTEP. Out of the way, lonely. Applied to a village or house.

OVERCLAP (E.) As to the weather. 'Will it vreeze to-night? It'll depend upon the overclap.' That is what may overclose the earth, as cloudiness.

OVES, Ovis. Eaves.

OVERLOOK, Auverlook. To look on with the evil eye.

OVERRIGHT, Auverright. Right over, against, opposite.

OWL. To owl about. Ramble by night.

P.

PALMER. A Palmer worm. A hairy worm.

PANK. To pant.

PANSHARD. A potsherd.

PANTILES. Ridge or roof tiles.

PAR. To confine or shut up. Also to surfeit.

PARRICK. A parrock, a small enclosed field, called in Queen's English 'a paddock,' which is an old word for a toad. The Dorset word is justified by the verb "Par," and by the Anglo-Saxon 'Pearroc,' and by old English and some forms of folk-speech. 'On thisum lytlum pearroce:'—*Alfred's Boethius*, xviii. 2.

  'Hadde pearrokod hymselve
  That no man might hym se?'
      Piers Plowman.

PASSEL (W.) A parcel.

PA'SONS AN CLARKS. The running fiery spots on burning paper.

PATCH (E.) A shield or cloke. 'Every one do love to put a patch on their own children.'

PEA (E.) The weight or bob of a steelyard.

PEALES. Railings.

PEANE. A pane as of glass and of some other flat spaces.

PEART. Lively, quick, pert.

PEAVIERS. Paving stones, flagstones.

PEAZE, Peze. To ooze out, as water through some earthen vessels or very small openings. 'The water pezed up vrom the ground at our he'th.'

PECK UPON. To hector over.

PELT. A fit of anger. 'He went off in sich a pelt.'

PEWITT. The lapwing.

PICK. A hay-fork or dung-fork.

PIERS, or Pyers. Hand rails of a foot bridge.

PILER. A tool consisting of many compartments, for pounding off the husk's of thrashed barley. (A.S. pilcre, *a pounder*.)

PILL (E.) A large brown pitcher.

PILLEM, Pelm (W.) Dust.

PIN. Pinbone.

PIN-SWEALE. A boil, or pimple.

PIRTY. Pretty. Pirty deäl. A great deal.

PISSABED. The dandelion, more especially the narrow dandelion (*leontodon taraxacum*), said to be very diuretic, whence its name in Dorset as in France.

PITCH. To put or throw up on a waggon. To subside as dirt in water. Sit down, 'Do ye pitch yourzelf in a chair.' To lay down 'pitchén' To sink down as a swelling or swollen stream. To pitch away and become thin from stout. 'She's a pitched away.'

PITCH. The quantity taken up at once on a pick or hayfork.

PITCHERS (Swanage.) Small square stones for pitching. The first work to which a quarry boy is set.

PITCHER. A pollard willow.

PITCHDEN PICK. A long handled and long pronged pick for putting up hay on the waggon or rick.

PLAIN. Middling. Far from being excellent or handsome. ''Tis but a plaïn crop.' 'He's a very plain man,' is an euphemismus for 'He is an ugly man.' Plain also means quite, as 'The wind is plaïn south.' Also homely without affectation, as 'How d'ye like Leädy A.?' 'Oh, very much; she's as plaïn as a deairymaïd.' 'I be but plaïn (W.) poorly, not well.'

PLAISTER. Plaster.

PLEAZEN. Places.

PLECK. A small enclosure. (A.S. plæc, a plat.)

PLESH, Plush, or Plash. To cut the larger sticks (pleshers, plushers, or plashers) of a quickset hedge nearly but not quite off, and lay them down on the bank, so that the sap may come up over the cut, and they may throw out shoots. Other handlings of a hedge are—To trim it: Cut it into good trim or shape. To shear it: Shear back only outreaching overgrowth. To rid out the hedge: Cut out all the wood that is not to be plushed.

PLIM. To swell. 'This beäcon do plim in bwilèn.'

PLOCK. A block. A large block of wood, particularly a 'choppèn plock,' for chopping up small wood upon.

PLOUGH, or Plow. A waggon is mostly called a plough, or plow, in the Vale of Blackmore, where the English plough, *aratrum*, is a zull, the Anglo-Saxon *syl*. 'These are in His Matie name to require you forthwith, on sight hereof, to press men and plowes.'—Colonel Kirk's order to the parish of Chedzoy, in the Monmouth rebellion.

PLOUNCE. To plunge down, as into water.

PLOW ROAD. A waggon or wheel road.

PLUFFY. Plumpy, stout.

PLY. To bend.

POCKFRETTEN. Marked by smallpox.

PODGY. Puggy, thick or big and short, big-bodied, as a fat man.

POLLARD TREE. A polled or beheaded tree.

POLLY WASH DISH, Polly Dishwasher (E.) The grey wagtail.

POMPEY. A name for a teakettle.

POMPER (E.) To promster, to poke or potter unskilfully on a disease or wound. 'We had better not pomper 'en ourselves, but call in a doctor.'

PONT. To poke, or strike, as an apple or fish, so hard that it begins to rot, or show the hue of rottenness, at the dint of the blow. 'His poor body wer like a ponted apple,' spoken of a boy who had fought and been beaten black and blue.

POOCH-PIE, Pouch-pie. A pie made of a flat round of paste doubled into a half circle with fruit, or meat within it. Mowers have sometimes a pouch for the whet-stone of this shape, of leather.

POOK. (*See* Haymeäken.)

POPE, Pwop. A big puppet. A term of reproach. 'What a *pwop* of a thing.'—Roberts' 'History of Lyme.'

POPE. A baby, thence a doll. Lat. Persius, Pupa, a doll.

POPPLES, or Popplestwones. Pebbles. (A.S. popolstàn.)

POPPY (E.) A dog, however old.

POSTES, Vistes, &c. The *e* ought to be allowed in English. Nothing can be worse than *sts* without a vowel in *posts* and *fists*.

POSTS of a Gate. The 'hangèn post' and the 'vallèn post.'

POT. A stick with a little basket of wicker-work on it, as a shield in cudgel-playing. Also a pannier.

POTT or Putt. A dung-pott, or dung-putt.

POUNCE. Applepounce. The ground apple for the cider wring. Pummice.

POUNSHALL. Punctual.

POUT. To poke out is sometimes spoken in E. Dorset of the hair, as 'How his heäir do pout.'

PRAISE, or Prize. To show forth by words or token. One said to another who showed tokens of pain in his leg—'You do seem to praïse your lag;' ah! (said he) 'He's so bad to day.' To praise a man as good is to praise him *up*. A prize is what is put forth by promise. When a horse is touched on a wounded or bruised part, he is säid to praïse pain or not, by flinching or otherwise.

PRICKET. Become sharp, as beer.

PRIDE-O'-THE-MARNEN. A foggy mist in the morning, likely to be followed by a warm day.

PROMP (W.) A prop.

PROOF. Fattening quality. Spoken of food. 'There's some proof in that hay.'

PROOFY. Having much proof, likely to fatten.

PROUD. Growing too fast and rank, as wheat may be.

PROVE. To fatten, to gain flesh.

PUCKER. A big poke or bag in cloth, badly sewed; also a poking about hastily as if to find something. 'She wer in such a pucker.'

PUD. A hand. 'Gie's a pud.'

PUDDING-STONE. Conglomerate, 'so styled because the stones and their matrix resemble pudding.'—*Roberts*.

PUDDLE. To mingle water with earth in planting.

PUG. To pull, poke.

PUGGY. 'A puggy man.'

PUMMEL-VOOTED. Club footed.

PUMMY. Apple-pummace from the cider wring.

PUMSTER (W.) To trifle with a disease; not calling in a physician.

PUNCH (W). To pont.

PURE. Quite well. "How b'ye?" "Pure, thenk ye."

PUR LAMB. A sound male lamb, a castrated ram lamb.

PUSH IN. (*See* Haymeäken).

PUSKY. Bloated.

A-PUT-OUT. Put out of one's usual temper; out of track; made angry.

A-PUT-TO. To be in a strait. "He's a-put-to vor money."

PUT TO TROUBLE. To prosecute one at law.

PUT UP. To stop for refreshment, or take board or bed at an inn. "Wher d'ye put up?" "At the Bell."

PUT UP WI'. To bear patiently. It is said of very wet or dry weather. "Well: we must put up wi' it," but without any bad feeling of impatience. "Who is to put up wi' your fancies?"

PUXY. A miry or boggy place; a puddle.

PWOPE, a Pope. A bunchy thing; an effigy. A Puppet is a small Pope.

PYER (see Piër). "Pyer and lug;" a rude bridge over a ditch, consisting of a pole (lug) to walk on, and a hand rail, (pyër.)

Q.

QUADDLE. To make limp or flabby, or shrivelled.

QUAG. A quagmire, which shakes when walked on.

QUAR. A stone quarry.

QUARREL. A window-pane.

QUARTEREVIL, or Quartere'il. A disease of sheep; a corruption of the blood.

QUEST, or Quist. Woodquest, a wood pigeon.

QUETTER. A working ulcer.

QUICKZET HEDGE. A planted living hedge, in distinction from a dead fence.

QUID. A cud.

QUINE. Coin. The corner of a wall.

QUIRK. To let out the breath suddenly and strongly after holding it, in strong work.

QUOB. To quiver like jelly.

QUONT. A boat pole. A stout pole forked at the outer end and used by fishermen of the fleet, by Portland, to push their flat-bottomed boats through passages or channels to the Chesil beach. I cannot see clearly whence the Fleet fisherman got the word. As *contus*, in Latin, means such a shoving pole, a friend hints that it might have come from the monks of Abbotsbury; but then I believe that we have to reckon with its use in Kent, if not elsewhere.

QUOT. Very low in proportion to its breadth. "There's a little quot rick."

R.

RACK. The under part of a barn's door, the upper one being called the door.

RACK (Reck N.) A broad frame of bars fastened up in old-fashioned houses, under a floor over head, where sundry things, as guns or flitches of bacon or others, were put up out of the way.

RAFT. To rouse one as when going to sleep or dying, or to raft a beast. "Teäke keäre. The cow's arafted. Teäke ceäre; she mid hook ye." In polite English the warning might be "The animal is infuriated. Take care, she may inflict on you some corporal injury."

RAFTY. Rancid, "Rafty beäcon."

RAKE. [A.S. réc-an.] To reek.

RAM. Ramish, strong smelling, rank.

RAMMIL. Rawmilk. Applied to cheese, made of raw unskimmed milk.

RAMSENS. Broad-leaved garlic *(allium ursinum)*.

RAM'S CLAWS. The stalks and stalk-roots of the creeping crowfoot *(ranunculus repens.)* The creeping crowfoot is often in the talk of haymakers where it is rife, as it catches the teeth of their rakes and sometimes breaks off one of them.

RAMSHACKLE. Loose-jointed and rickety.

RAM-STAG. A castrated ram.

RAND, Ran, or Run. The hank of a string. A length of twine.

RANDY. A merry-making; an uproar.

RANGLE. To reach about like trailing or climbing plants.

RAP. To barter; to exchange articles. "I've a-rapped awoy the hoss."

RAPPEN. Out-reaching; big.

RATCH. To stretch.

RATE. To scold; to accuse. "Thæt hig wrehton hyne."—*Mat.* XII. 10. "And foule y-rebuked. And *a-rated* of rich men."—*Piers Plowman*.

RATHE. [A.S. bræthe.] Soon; early. Thence "rathripe" the name of an apple. "Sometimes more *rathe* thou risest in the east."—*Ovid's Metamorph*.

RATHER. Lately; just now. "He's rather a-come." Thence "I wou'd rather do so:" *i.e.* "I would sooner do so," or "do so sooner than otherwise."

RATHERIPE. Early ripe, as spoken of fruit.

RAWN, or Rean. To raven or reach in food eagerly. "How the hoss do rawn in the hay."

RAY. To array, put on raiment; to dress.

RAYEN-ZIEVE. A sieve, used chiefly in cleansing clover.

READ. [A.S. hredan, to rid, pull.] To read inwards, is to strip them of their fat, &c.

READ. (20.) The fourth stomach of ruminant animals. The masticated food of ruminant animals passes into the first stomach —*paunch*—and second—*honeycuombbag*—where it is formed into cuds and sent back to the mouth to be chewed again. The third stomach to which it next goes down is in Dorset the *fadge*, from which it goes on to the *read*, or fourth. These last words are further examples of the fullness of the rustic dialect where English is defective; for in an English translation of Cuvier's "Animal Kingdom," the *fadge*, for want of an English name as it is fair to believe, is called by its French one, the *feuillet*, or bookleaf, from its dissepiments which are like the leaves of a book; and the *read* is given as the *caillette*. A calve's read salted in water is used to curdle milk.

REAKE, or Reaky. To reäke a'ter plough. To rake after the waggon at loading in the hayfield.

REAMES. A skeleton; the frame or ligaments of a thing. "Here be the reämes of a bird."

REAMY. That may be pulled out without breaking, like hot toasted cheese. Spoken of slack bread.

REAN (N). (*See* Rawn.)

REAP. There are known three ways of cutting wheat—reaping (reapèn), hewing (hewèn), haming (hamèn). 1. Reaping or handcutting: The cutting of a grip or handfull at a time by drawing in of the sickle through it. 2. Hewing is, I believe, the hewing or chopping back of the wheat against the standing corn, enough together to make a sheaf. 3. Haming: The cutting and taking back against the forward leg—shielded by a strip of wood—corn enough for a sheaf. Haming is mostly taken from the Saxon *ham*, home, which means close up, as the knife went in home to the haft. So in haming, the cutter brings the corn home to himself. I believe hewèn is called in Devon, and W. Dorset youghing.

REAR. To raise; to rouse; to excite. "You'll rear the weather" is sometimes said to one who, for a wonder, comes to help in the hay field.

REARAGE (C.) The number of sheep reared on a farm in one year.

REAVES. The ladder-like framework attached to the sides of a waggon to uphold the load over the wheels. The reäves are propped by strouters, or stretchers.

REDDICK, Reddock, Ruddock. The robin-redbreast.

REDESHIP. Reasoning, or ground of good reasoning. "You've a-put the knives across. We shall quarrel." "Ah! there idden much redeship in that."

REDROUGHS (E.) Scarlet runners (French beans).

REDWEED. The poppy.

REED. Wheat straw drawn for thatching.

REEF. A broad reaching piece. "They've a-mowed sich a reef o' groun' to-day."

REELLY. To dance reels.

REEM. To stretch out, broaden, or lengthen. "I'll walk out to reem my lags."

REER, or Rare. [A.S. hrere.] Underdone, as meat.

REEVE (E.) To unravel, as a piece of knitting.

RENGE. A hair sieve for flour or liquor.

REREMOUSE. A bat. ("Midsummer Night's Dream" ii. 3.)

RICE. Brushwood.

RICK. A stack or mow with a sharp ridge or a pointed top.

RICK. A. S. Hreac or hricg, a pinnacle. "Gesette hine ofer thæs temple's *hricg*."—*Luke 4, 9*.

RID out a hedge. To cut or clear out unnecessary wood in laying or pleashing of a hedge.

RIDE. To be angry when teazed or jeered. "I meàde en ride."

RIDDLE. [A.S. Hriddell a kind of coarse sieve. "Satanas gyrnde thæt he eow *hridrode* swa-swa hwæte."—*Luke 22, 31*.

RIDS. Reds.

RIFF-RAFF.

RIG. To climb about. "Zit down! a riggén about zoo." To roam about out of the way.

RIG, or Rudger. An uncastrated horse.

RIGGY, Riggish. Sour.

RIGHTS. A right state. "To put to rights" is to mend or repair.

RILE. To reach about as a restless child.

RIMER. A reemer. A tool for enlarging screw holes in metal. (*See* Reem).

RINE. Rind.
> "The gray moss marred his *ryne*."
> *Spenser's Shepherd's Calendar.*

RINGLE. To ring with a small sound. "I heärd the glass ringle when the winder wer a-broke."

RISE. To raise; to get.

RIVE. A rank smell, as that of a fox or badger.

RIVELLED, Rifled. Shrivelled as grass.
> "She cast
> Her old wive's *riveled* shape away.—*Ovid's Metam.*

ROACH. Rough, coarse, rank.

ROBINHOOD. The Red Campion *(lychnus dioica)* and the Ragged Robin *(lychnus flos cuculi)*.

ROLL-ER. See Häymeäken. Roll-er also means a roll of wool. When wool was hand-carded the quantity carded at once was rolled off the cards in a little roll called a roll-er, from the weakness of which came the saying "I'm so weak as a roll-er." The "o" in roll-er has the sound of "o" in collar.

RONG. A rung, meaning also a cudgel or walking staff. The rundle or step of a ladder.

ROSOM (W.) A saw or proverb.

ROTTLEPENNY. The yellow rattle *(rhinanthus christigalli).*

ROTTLETRAPS. Rickety old household goods, &c.

ROUETS. Tufts of rough grass.

ROUGH. Uneasy, or in pain. "I be but rough to-day."

ROUGHCAST, or Roücast. To cover walls, particularly mud walls, with roughcast—a composition of sand, mortar, grit, &c.

ROUGHLEAF. A true leaf of a plant, in distinction from its seed leaves or *cotyledons*. When its first true leaves are out it is said to be "out in rough leaf."

ROUNDERS. A boys' game at balls.

ROUT. A rut.

Row, or Roo. To push in hay in weäling. (*See* Hâymeäkèn).

ROWSE. To drive off, scare away. "Rowse the vowls out o' geärden."

ROWSE. A noise. "The bees be good when they do meäke a rowse."

RUDDER, or Ruddle. (*See* Riddle.)

RUDDER, or Rudern-sieve. A sieve for cleaning wheat.

RUDDLE. A red earth by which they mark sheep.

RUDDOCK. The Robin redbreast.

RUDGE-TIE, or Ridge-tie. A chain lying over the ridge tree to hold up the shafts of a waggon or cart.

RUDGER. (*See* Rig.)

RUF. A roof.

RUGGLE, or Ruckle. To rock or roll about. Also to wheel as a barrow.

RUM. Queer.

RUMSTICK. A queer man.

RUNDLEWOOD, Randlewood. The small sticks from the head of a tree ripped of bark. The larger ones are called lagwood.

RUN DOWN. To depreciate; to find fault with; to speak ill of. The Dorset dialect often affords good examples of running down, particularly of work—not from the ill nature of its speakers, but from a wish to show their own skill. The following samples are from life:—"Well; what d'ye think o' the new waggon?" "Why, the vust thing I do vine fate wi' is the drats; tha be too crooked: and the tug-irons be a-put in mwore than dree inches too vur back. An' jis' look here, where the rudge-tie and breechèn rings be: why, nar a carter in the wordle can't put a hoss into en. I don't call the head and tail a-put out 'o han' well. They be a-painted noo-how. Why 'e woon't bear hafe a luoad; tha've a-meäde en o' green stuff a-shook all to pieces. The vust time 'e 's a-haled out in the zun, e'll come all abrode. The strongest thing I do zee about en is the mâinpin; and he is too big by hafe." And so on. "What did ye gi'e var they vish?" "Two-pence a-piece." "Lawk! how dear they be. Why I wou'den gi'e a penny for the lot. Why they be a-ponted an' a-squotted all to pieces: they woon't keep till to-morra."

S.

SAMMEL (N.) A gutty, sandy earth mingled with soft stuff.

SAMMEL, Sammy. A silly, simple fellow.

SAMEL, Sammy. Simy, Simon; Simple, Simpleton. Have nothing to do with the name of Samuel or Simon. They come from a stemword, *Sam* (s—m), meaning a body of soft matter. Seam, Lard, and Samsodden, meaning boiled to a soft stuff, are forms of it.

SAR. To serve or feed animals.

SARCH. Search.
> "March 'ull sarch,
> Eäpril 'ull try,
> Mäy 'ull tell
> If you'll live or die."
> A saying of health and weather.

SARCH. A fine hair sieve for meal. (Sarse: Bayley.)

SASSY. Saucy.

SA'T, Sate (N.) Soft.

SA'TPOLL (N.) Soft poll, soft head, silly one.

SAY. A slight trial. "Oone säy, two säy, dree and away," the säy being a slight movement or running.

SCALLOPS. The refuse of lard.

SCAMMISH. Awkward, scram.

SCANCE (S.E.) Skeat (E.) A looseness of the bowels, diarrhœa in cattle. (*See* skent).

SCOOP, Scoopens. Scope. Law of ground given by one to another running against him.

SCOTE. To shoot along very fast, as in running.

SCRAG. A very crooked branch of a tree.

SCRAGGY. Having many scrags.

SCRAGGLE. To walk with the legs and body very crooked, as a cripple.

SCRAM, Screwy, awkward. "How scram he do handle it."

SCRAM (W). Screwy grown, dwarfish.

SCRAPE. A sheep-scrape, a bare place, where the turf has been scraped off by sheep's feet on a steep down-side.

SCREED. To shun, to eschew.

SCREAK. To creak loudly.

SCRIDDICK. A small scrap or shred.

SCRIMPY. Scrimp-like, screwy, shrivelled, as half starved.

SCRIP. A hedger's or shepherd's coat, sometimes made of leather.

SCROFF. Small bits of dead wood fallen under trees, or leavings under piles, or from faggots.

SCROOP, Scroopy. To give a low sound of one hard body scraping on another. If it is a shrill sound it is rightly a creaking. If shrill and very strong a screaking. If low it is a scrooping.

SCROUGE. To screw or squeeze up.

SCROUNCH, or Scrunch. To crunch much or strongly. "The dog do scrunch the bwone."

SCRUSH, Scrouge. To crush much.

SCRUSH. A game, much like shinty, between two sides of boys, each with bandies (scrushes), trying to knock a roundish stone over the other's line.

SCUD. A short slight shower cast from a flying cloud, a passing shower.

SCUD. To shoot forth swiftly. "Wheather doe ye scud from death's fit." "Stonyhurst" (Virgil).

SCUFF. To shove the foot along the floor or ground after putting it down in walking, like one slip-shod.

SCUFF of the neck. The bare part of the neck close below the hair, and sometimes called the scroff of the neck.

SCUFFLE (W.) A shoving about, a slight fighting or struggle.

SCUTE. A reward, pay, scot.

SCWÖOE. To barter or exchange.

SEATED. Applied to eggs, having been sitten on, with the formation of the young bird begun.

SEAVE the hây. "To seäve the hây wi' the maïdens" is to cover them over with hay in play.

SEEM an I. Seems to me.

SESS, SISS. An exhortation to a dog to set him on somebody, or something.

SET OUT. An outset, a starting, or a proceeding. "A pirty set-out." "A pretty proceeding, or start."

SETTY (E.) Spoken of eggs. Eggs on which the hen has sitten some while.

SETTLE. A long bench with a high planken back.

SEW. (*See* Azew).

SHAB. The itch, applied to brutes.

SHABBY.

SHAB OFF. To go off softly as ashamed.

SHACKLEN (W.N.) Loose limbed, lazy, as if shackle-boned, shaking about.

SHAKE. A crack in timber.

SHALE. To take off the shell; as, to shale beans or nuts.

SHANDY (W.) As a bough that shies back from the stroke of the hook, and must be holden to it to be cut off.

SHARD (W.) A broken piece, or a breach; as a panshard, a piece of broken pan; or a shard, a small breach in a hedge. (*See* Gap).

SHARK, or Shirk off. To sneak off softly, from shame or an apprehension of danger.

SHARPS. The shafts of a cart or other carriage.

SHARPS. A fine kind of bran.

SHATTEN. Shall not.

SHATTER. To shed about in small quantities, as of hay or other loose stuff.

SHEAKES. "Noo girt sheakes." "No great things;" nothing to brag of.

SHEAR. A ploughshare. Also, a crop of grass.

SHEEN. To shine.

SHEEP. The Dorset sheep, sometimes so called, are a fair, horned kind. We may say of the Southdowns and Dorset sheep as Pliny (Nat. Hist. L 8, c 47) writes of two kinds:—

"Illud genus mollius,
   Hoc in pascua elegantius."

Those a finer wool may yield,
But these are fairer in the field.

SHEPHERDESS (E.) The yellow wagtail.

SHEETED. A sheeted cow is one having a white band, like a sheet round the body.

SHIRK. To sheer off, shun. (*See* Shark.)

SHITTLE-EXE. A timber of a waggon, taking the summers.

SHOCKLE (N.), Shackle (W.) To shake about lightly, as marbles in a boy's pocket, or ripe seeds in a dry capsule.

SHOCKLY. That shockles.

SHOCKLE-APPLE. An apple so ripe that the pips can be heard to shockle or shake about.

SHOD (W.) To shed.

SHON'T. Shall not.

SHOO. A cry to fray away fowls.

SHOOK. Split; as wood by shrinking.

SHOOT. A steep hill, or the road down it.

SHOLDUERENS. Cider from shoulderings means from stolen apples carried home on the shoulders.

SHOTTEN. Shalt not.

SHOULD. I would give a few words on a use of this word in a Dorset idiom, as a gentleman who came to live in Dorset about ten years ago writes that he has never heard the wording out of Dorset, and that his mind was at first much struck by it, and he would call to it the attention of your Dorset readers. The wording is as this:—"I'm atwuold that you *should zay* that I ben't very sprack" (brisk, as at work.) You should say, not you say; and why so? and does it mean "you ought to say?" I understand that it comes from an ellipsis of other words. A friend may say to me "Between ourselves what do you think of A?" And I may answer "I *should say* that he is not over sprack." This would be less bold and harsh than "I say he is not over sprack"; yet that might be far too strong for my knowledge of A, and "I should say" means "I should say so, if I must give an opinion." So the whole wording seems to be "I am told that you (say that you) should say, if you must give your opinion of me, that I am not over sprack."

SHOVE. A rough rowling of the sea.

SHOWL. A shovel.

SHOWANCE. Something to show as a proof, such as a written note

SHRAM. A screwing up or out of the body and limbs from keen cold.

SHRIMPY. Thin, arid, poor. Applied to land.

SHROCROP. The shrewmouse. It is thought, in some parts of Dorset, that if it runs over one's foot it will make one lame. It may not seem clear what a shrewmouse has in common with a woman shrew. The shrewmouse gives a shrill, shreaking sound, and I believe the shrew is so called from her shrill, shreaking voice in scolding.

SHROUD. To lop or prune the heads (shrouds) of timber trees. "With a shadowing shroud."—Ezekiel xxxi. 3.

SHROUDED. Shrunk or curled up, as newly set plants, by heat.

SHROVY. "To goo a-shrovèn" is to go a-begging at Shrovetide.

SHROVY. Poor, mean. Applied to land.

SHROWROD (S.E.) Shrewridden lameness if overrun by a shrew-mouse.

SHUT. To join, as to weld two pieces of iron, or connect two pieces of wood; to agree. "We two can't shut." To shut back. Push back, as a cart by the horse.

SHUT OUT, or Shut off. "To shut out, or shut off work." "To leave off work." Comp. the Latin *concludo*, to shut up.

SHUT BACK. Shoot or push back. Spoken to a horse.
of hand or a receipt.

SIFY (W.) To catch the breath in sighing; to sob.
SIGHT. "Sich a zight o' vok," or anything else, means such a number or quantity.
SILGREEN. Houseleck (*sempervivum tectorum.*) Its leaves are thought to be cooling, and are used with cream for the blood.
SINGLE CASTLE. The *Orchis moris* and *mascula* (Portland).
SIPPET. A little sop.
SITH. To sigh.
SIVE. A Scythe.
SIVES. Chives; garlic (*allium schœnoprasum*), used as a potherb.
SKAFFEL, Sceäfel. Waste chips or cuttings from the dressing or making, so called (?) of the blocks of stone at the quarries, Portland. From Anglo-Saxon scæfian, to shave or cut off.
SKENT. Looseness in the bowels. Applied to cattle.
SKENT (E.) The diarrhœa in cattle.
SKEW (M).
SKEW-WHIFF. A-skew, a-skant.
SKICER. A lamb that runs over much.
SKIDDLE (W.) To cut up wastefully.
SKIFF. Askew; awkward (as left-handed), skiff-handed; having a distorted hand.
SKILLEN. A penthouse; a shed.
SKILLET. A big thick kind of saucepan, mostly of bell-metal, with a long handle.
"A bellmettel skillet, 2s. 6d."
A Dorset Inventory, 1729.
"Some ran a goodly trot
With a skillet or a pot."
SKILLY. Scaly, niggardly.
SKIM, or Skimmy. To mow the bunches of rank grass in a summerleaze.
SKIT. To run or walk lightly; to shoot on.
SKIVER. A skewer; a shaving or shiver of wood.
SKIVER-WOOD. Spindle-tree (*euonymus Europœus*), of which skewers are made.
SKRAM. (*See* Scram).
SKURRICK, or Skurrock. [A.S. scearan.] A small share. "Every skurrick o't." "Every bit, every farthing of it."
SLACK-TWISTED. Inactive; lazy. Applied to a person.

SLAIT, or Slade. [A.S. slaed.] A sheepslâit; a sheep-plain or down; a sheepleaze.

SLAT. A slate.

SLAT (N.), Slate (S.E.) The young and as yet flat pod as of the pea. "The peas be out in slat."

SLAT (W.) To fling down carelessly. Also kidding or podding, as peas.

SLATCH. To slake; to make slack, as lime by water.

SLENT. To tear as linen. Also a slit.

SLEEPY. Very loose or slack, as a rotten apple.

SLIDES of a waggon: Felloe-pieces or arcs of circles fastened on the fore axle, as a bearing for the bed of the waggon when it locks.

SLIM. Slender. "What a slim chap."

SLIM. Sly; scowling.

SLINGERS (W.) Fir cones.

SLIP. A cord or chain, to fasten a cow's neck to the tying in a stall.

SLIPS. Young weaned pigs running loose. Those somewhat older are hard slips; and others nearly full-grown are store pigs.

SLOMMOCK. A slatternly woman.

SLOMMOCKEN. Dirty, or slatternly.

SLOO. A sloe.

SLOO, of a horn. The inner bony prominence from the skull or quick core of a cow's horn, fitting, as it were, into a socket of it. It bleeds when broken.

SLOOWORM. The Slow-worm, or blind-worm.

SLUCK-A-BED. A sluggard.

SLUGGARD'S GUISE. A sluggard's manner.
"Sluggard's guise,
Lwoth to goo to bed, an' lwoth to rise."

SMAME. To smear.

SMAMER. A flat blow, a smack. "I'll gi'e thee a smamer," a good smack in the face.

SMATCH. A taste, a smack.

SMATTER. A mess.

SMEECH, or Smeitch. A cloud of dust.

SMELL. "The plants will be finish here when they do smell the manure." "Do smell very warm here." Some might say. plants cannot smell, as they have not noses; but smell, a noun, and not a verb, means that fine matter which flows from a thing to the nose, as what we call a smell good or bad, and to smell manure or a flower is to take in its smell—the matter so called.

SMOCK-FROCK. A man's round frock of linen.

SMOOR. To smear.

SNABBLE. To snap up hastily or greedily.

SNAG. The small peabig variety or species of sloe. Most writers on wortlore seem to take the snag thorn as only a variety of the sloe thorn, and call it "*Prunus Spinosa.*" A lady from London, who was staying at a Dorset house, came, as she walked through a field, upon some children picking snags, and said to them "Oh! so you are gathering sloes." "No, Mêm; they ben't sloos, they be snags," was the answer. The lady went on her way with an English name for the fruit of the *Prunus B.*

SNAG (W.) Variety.

SNAGS, Stumps. Thence the snags or stumps of trees washed down by the rivers of America, and sticking up above or sometimes a little under water, and likely to hit a hole in the boat: in provision for which accident the Americans have built boats with water-tight compartments at the bow, called snag-chambers.

SNAKEFLOWER. The windflower, *anemone nemorosa.*

SNAP (W.) Snap a small taking of food.

SNAPE. A spring.

SNAPY. Springy; wet. Said of land.

SNAPPEN TONGS. A game of forfeits.

SNAPPISH. Wont to snap or snub off another's talk; short, angry answers.

SNEAD. The pole of a scythe; in Dorset zive, or sive. The scythe is fixed to the sneäd by a steart, that goes into a socket, and by a ring—king-ring, and wedges—king-wedges. Upon the sneäd are two short crooked handles—tugs, or tinestocks. That part of the blade nearest the sneäd is its heel.

SNIGGER. To smile or laugh sillily, as if with a sneer.

SNIGGLE. To snort a little.

SNIGGLE. To cut in small nicks or notches.

SNIPE (W.) The nose or peak of a boy's cap.

SNOATCH. To speak or breathe hardly through the nose.

SNOCK. A smart knock; a short sound of a sudden blow.

SNOFF. A candle-snuff. Also, the eye of an apple.

SNOFF. A youth was going to snuff a candle with fingers. His friend, a wit, said, "Now, be your vingers clean enough to snoff en?"

SNORTER, Snatter. The bird wheat-ear (Portland).

SNOTCH. A wide notch.

SNOUT. To snub or snap off a speaker in a gruff tone.

SNOUTISH. Wont to snout.

SOG. To soak or loosen with wet. Spoken of land, or a road.

SOGGY. Soaky, water-soaked. Spoken of ground.

SOJER. Soldier, the *pyrochroa rubens*.

SOLID, Solid. Also serious or gentle; "She do look solid." "Come solid, goo sassy."

SOMEWHEN. At some time.

SOONERE. A ghost.

SO'S [Cornish sos.] Souls, meaning folks or men in distinction from brutes. "O so's!" "O folks!"

SO'T. Soft.

SO'TPOLL [O.E. poll, the head; thence a poll-tax, a capitation tax; to poll, to count heads, as of voters; and a pollard, a beheaded tree.] A silly person; a soft poll. To say one has a soft-poll is, in Blackmore, the same as saying that he has a weak mind.

SOWEL, or Sole. A sharp shore or stake, such as is driven into ground to fasten up hurdles to. Same as seäle.

SPAN-NEW. "Spick-an'-span new;" "Quite new; wholly new." Span-new, as is shown by the Icelandic spánnyr, of the same meaning, is chip-new; as, a thing made of timber, and not yet removed from among its chips. From spán, a chip or wooden spoon, of our Teutonic forefathers, might come our spoon; so that "chips and porridge" might not have been barely imaginary with them.

SPARBILLS. A kind of nails used in shoes.

SPARGADS. Gads, or sticks, to be split up into spars. (*See* Gad).

SPARHOOK. A small bill-hook for making or cutting of spars.

SPARS. Sharp sticks, usually of withy or hazel, twisted in the middle and bent, for fastening down thatch under ledgers.

SPARKED. Marked with at least one white spark; a peaked mark like a spearhead, not a round spot. If you cast ink from a pen plump on paper you will make a spot, if very slantingly a spark.

SPAWL. A splinter flown off, as from stone.

SPEAK an' deäb (spike and daub?): A wall of wattles or hurdle-work plastered over with mortar. We may well believe that wattle walling was chosen by the early Britons in house building. The Welsh word for building is now *Adeilo* from *Eilo*, to put alternately, to plait, wreathe. "Solomon a adeiladodd dy iddo ef," Solomon built to him a house—Acts vii. 47. By root meaning "Solomon wattled to him a house."

SPEAKER. A long shoulder stake on which to carry a nitch of wood.

SPEARDE. A spade. The stem of a spade is called the tree, and the cross handle on its top the critch.

SPEARE. Thin. "He's a very speäre man."

SPEARS. The stems of the reed *arundo phragmites*, sometimes employed instead of laths to hold plaster. In I. of Wight spires are the tall blades of the *carex paniculata* and other lofty sedges.

SPET. To spit. "Spets on his napkin"—*Scoloker's Diaphanthus, 1604*. Gent. Mag., Sept., 1841.

SPIK, Spike. Lavender.

SPILES (N.) The beard of barley.

SPINDLE OUT. To begin to grow into stalks or spindles. Spoken of young corn-plants.

SPINE. The coming turf of ground lately sown down to grass.

SPIRT. To sprout; to vegetate.

SPITISH. Spiteful; snappish.

SPITTER. A dock-spitter, or thistle-spitter; a tool to cut up docks or thistles.

SPLEENISH (W.) Wild, headlong, splunging; a spleenish chap.

SPOOL. A winding spindle for spinning.

SPRACK. Lively, springy, active.

SPREADER. (*See* Stratcher).

SPRETHE. To chap. "My lips be a-sprethed."

SPRING. Crack open as unseasoned board.

SPRY. Strong of muscle and springy, as in bodily games.

SPUDDLE. To dig slightly and incontinuously. "To spuddle teäties," is to turn up ground out of which potatoes have been dug, to find left ones.

SPUDGEL. A hollow kind of shovel for baling out of water. Also, to bale.

SPUR. "To spur dung" is to throw it abroad from the heaps left by the dung-putt.

SQUAIL. To throw stones or any missiles at birds or other things.

SQUINCH (N.) As of tea or salt, as much as can be taken (squeezed) up between the thumb and forefinger. "Can ye lend me a squinch o' tea."

SQUIT. To make a very short slight sound. "I heärd the cat 'squit' droo the glass."

SQUITTERS (E.) The diarrhœa in cattle.

SQUOT. To flatten as by a blow.

SQUOT. To make very quot.

STADDLE. A wooden frame-work, or a bed of boughs, upon which a rick is made so as not to touch the ground.

STADDLEN, Staddling. Stuff to make a staddle.

STAID, in years. Elderly.

STAIRVOOT. The bottom of the stairs.

STALL. A cowstall or cribhouse, in which bullocks are fed, being fastened by loose *slips* round their necks to—*tyèns*—upright poles behind the cribs. They are sometimes served from behind, and sometimes from a passage—*forestall*—running on before the cribs.

STAN' BY. To stand by one's word is to be true to it. To stand by a man is to stand by him as a friend with help. *Adsisto* (Latin), whence comes assist, is of the same meaning.

STAN' TO. To stan' to a chile; to be sponsor. To stan' to an assertion; to insist on it.

STARE. A starling.

STARRY. A story.

STEAN. To pave or furnish with stones. "A good steäned road."

STEAN. An old cheese-press consisted of a frame with a shelf, upon which the vat (veät) was put. The cover of the vat was the vollier, which was wrung down upon the cheese by a great box of stones called the steän.

STEARE. To stay stiff. "How the ho'sses heair do steäre," stand stiff instead of lying down sleek.

STEART. A sharp point; a tail. Hence the red-start, a bird with a red tail.

STEER (E.) A stir; uproar.

STEM. The handle of a pick or rake. Also, a stretch of time.

To STEMMY. To work or take on in turns, or stems, with another; to take one's turn.

STICK. A tree is often called a stick. "That's a fine stick."

STICKLAND (Stickle land.) Steep land. Name of a Dorset parish.

STICKLE. Steep. "Theös hill is rather stickle."

STICK'S-END. The unburnt end of a stick from the fire.

STITCH. A set of sheaves stuck up in the field, top to top.

STIVER. To stiffen up much as an angry dog's hairs.

STOCKY. Thick of growth.

STODGE. Over thick, if not, sticky mud or spoon meat.

STOMACHY. High-minded when insulted.

STOOLS. The roots of copse or hedgewood cut down nearly to the ground.

STOOR. To stir, as a liquid.

STOUT. The cowfly, *Tabanus bovinus*.

STRAMER. A great skam, or overstraining of the truth, as in boasting or otherwise of the less blameworthy form of a hyperbole. The following heard by me may be a sample of a little skam:—Woman, to another, about the noisy friends of a neighbour just confined, whom they had come to see: "They were a-bouncèn out an' in, an' a-lafèn an' a-talkèn zoo that I thought they'd beat the house down." (2.) "Lauk! if I'd a-been in her pleäce it would a-drove me up drough the ceilèn."

STRAMOTE. A stalk of grass.

STRAPPEN. Of great size.

STRAPPER. A helping labourer hired only for a busy time.

STRATCH. Stretch. "An hour upon stretch."

STRATCHER, or Spreader. A stick to keep out the traces from the horses' legs.

STRÆK. One strip of the bond of a wheel.

STRAWEN, Strawing, or Strewing. A strawing of potatoes, is the set of potatoes or stalks growing from one mother-tuber.

STRENT. Same as slent.

STREECH. The space taken in at one striking of the rake. Streech measure is that in which a straight stick is struck over the top of a vessel.

STUBBERD. An early kind of apple.

STUD. A steadfast stillness of body, as of one in thought.

STUMP. To become stiff or sturdy or sulky.

STUMP, Stumpy. To walk with short stamping steps.

STUMPY. Short and thick. "A stumpy chap."

STUNPOLL, Stonehead, Stunhead. A blockhead. Also, an old half-dead tree.

SUENT. Smooth and even.

SUMPLE. Supple.

SWANSKIN. A very thick and close woollen cloth or flannel, formerly made at Sturminster Newton, mainly for the wear of fishermen out in Newfoundland.

SWEAL, Zwele. To scorch.

SWEAT. Zweat.

SWEEM, ZWIM. A sickly giddiness of the head (vertigo), a feeling as of a swinging round of the head. In Welsh, Pendro head-turning. It is from a wide spread Teutonic root. Saxon and Friesic swima. Saterland, swime. Iceland, svim. It formerly meant a swooning. "My head do zwim."

SWEEMY, Zweemy, Sweemish, Zweemish. Feeling a sweem in the head. "I wer sweemish all day eesterday." The old Friesic laws marked three forms of swima as swoonings from a blow in the head—(1.) That in which a man falls and rises without help, (2.) In which he lies helpless for a while, (3.) In which he lies lifeless or without hope of health.

SWEEP. A curve.

SWEETHEART. A lover.

SWIFT. A wheel for spinning of hemp.

SWIPES. Very thin beer.

SWOP. To barter, chop.

SWOP. A strong whop.

SWORD of a dung putt, an upright bar with holes for a pin, by which the putt is set at any pitch to shoot the manure.

T.

TACK. A shelf outreaching from the wall.

TACKLE. To manage; cope with; to undertake; to be a match for. "I can tackle you any day." "I could tackle a pint o' beer."

TAFFETY. Dainty or nice of food.

TAFFLE. To tangle somewhat, as grass or corn beaten down by weather.

TAILEN. Small corn driven farther from the middle of the heap to the tail of it; in winnowing; mostly used at home.

TAIL-ON-END. Eager to do anything; setting at it with liveliness; a figure taken from an eager dog.

TAIT. To play at see-saw. [A.S. Tihtan, to draw, pull.]

TAKE. A whitlow.

TALLET. A hay loft over a stable. Some think that tallet comes by wordshortening from "The hay loft." But if it were so, then, by Grimm's law, the hay knife would have become tannif. The Hayrick: T'Harrick, and the Hayrope: Tarrop.

TAMY, Tammy. Stretchsome; stringy; like toasted cheese that will stretch somewhat without breaking.

TARBLE, Tarblish. Tolerable; pretty well or good.

TARDLE. To tangle much.

TARVATCH, Tervatch. Tarvetch: A species of tare *(ervum)* that grows among the corn and in wet weather weighs it down. Most likely the wort which in old works is called the T'arefytche. (*See* "Prior's names of British plants.")

TEAGUISH. Fretful.

TEAKE AFTER. To take in shape, or looks, or behaviour after another. "He do teäke after his father."

TEAKE ON. To begin. This is just the Latin wording in the word *incipio, incapio* from *in, on,* and *capio*—to take.

TEAKE TO. To reach forth, to a man or thing with a ready good will. "Do the children teäke to their school?" "Do the 'prentice teäke to his treäde?" "The dog do teäke to his new meäster."

TEAKE VOR. Take for; to take the way for. "The heäre took vor the wood."

TO TEAKE OFF. To draw; make a drawing of. "He took off the church." These wordings which are good English, become clearer on our knowing that the word take, Saxon taec-an, meant at first to reach forth. If you take an apple from the table you (1) reach forth the hand to it, (2) you close your fingers on it, (3) you nighen or bring back your hand with it. The truer word for the first of the deeds is *take*, which we use for all three of them. The truer word for the third was Saxon *nim-an*, German *nehm-en* to nighen to himself, which the Germans have kept for all three, as "wollen sie einen apfel nehmen." Will you take an apple? Saxon, "Nimath min geoc ofér eow. Take my yoke ofer you," Matt. xi. 29. In Friesic, "Nim myn yok op yimme."

A Took To. To be taken to is to be overtaken by some stronger power as justice or the law or some Nemesis, like a wicked man, as "He's a took to at last."

Teaken. A taking, an agitation, a reaching about of the limbs and body from strong feeling. "She wer in sich a teäkèn."

Teare. Very eager and bold in onset, as flies on cattle or matter of food. "How teäre the vlees be."

Teart. Tart sharp, as a "Teärt meäster" or "A teärt cheese, a stingy cheese." [A.S. teart.]

Teave. To reach about the limbs in struggling wise, like a restless child. "The child do teäve zoo that I can't ray en."

Ted. (*See* Haymeäkèn).

Tee Hole. The door hole of the beepot.

Teery. Tanging out long and weak, spoken of plants.

Teg, (Sussex) Tagge. A lamb from one year old till its first shearing time.

Tell. To reckon.
"And ev'ry shepherd tells his tale
Under the hawthorn in the dale." *Milton.*

Terrible. Used for Very.

Tet, Tetty. A teat.

Tetchy, Touchy. Irritable.

Tewly, Tewl. Small and weakly, spoken of a child or a plant. *That* is sometimes used for *so* "I be that tired that I can hardly put oone voot avore tother."

Thatchen. Some of the thatcher's tools are by name the "shearèn hook;" "bittle," a little flat beetle to smooth down the thatch. His "hand-leathers," to ward the hands from sharp edges of the reed, and "knee-knaps or leather caps" over the knees.

Thaut, Thwart? The bench of a boat (Portland).

Theave. A sheep three years old.

Theosem. These.

Therence. Thence.

Thereright. Just there, without leaving the spot. (French) "Sur le champ."

Thick. Close in friendship. "So thick as inkle weavers." Inkle being only a kind of tape would call only for a very narrow loom, and the weavers might be close side by side.

Thicked Milk. Milk thickened with flour and boiled.

THIK (Th soft as in thee.) That.

THILLER. Thill horse. (Saxon—Thil; a pole or shaft.) The shaft or wheel horse of a team.

THILL HARNESS. The harness of the thiller.

THIRTOVER, Thwart over. Perverse. Thwartsome to others. "So overthwart as this." (Poems by the Duke of Orleans.)

THOROUGHPOLE. (*See* Waggon).

THREE-CUNNEN (W.) Over sharp.

TIDE. The tides or times of year were formerly given by the times of some of our then great fairs. Woodbury tide was given in a court roll as that of some custom on the common land of the manor.

TIDD'N'. 'Tis not.

'T ANDRE's TIDE (St. Andrew's tide.) Milborne St. Andrew's fair.

TILT. What is set up. High anger, as that of wounded pride. "She wer in sich a tilt," or "She wer zoo azet up."

TILT BONNET (W.) A garden bonnet without stuffing.

TILTY, Tiltish. Soon heated into a tilt or "set up."

TIMMERSOME. Restless, spoken of a child.

TINE. To hedge in ground. [A.S. Tynan.] To hedge in, enclosed by a fence. Whence tún a garden, homestead, farm, now a town. In composition-ton as Maiden Newton.

TINE. To kindle as a fire or candle.

TINES. Teeth of a harrow.

TINESTOCKS. (*See* Snead

TIP (a rick.) To make its top sharp. This is done by pulling of loose hay from its side, and by cutting of it round the bottom, and tipping of it with the hay thus gotten.

TISS, Tess. To hiss strongly, as a cat, or as water cast on red hot iron.

TISTYTOSTY. A child's toss ball of cowslips.

TITTERY (W.) Untrim, unstable. Rather tottery or shaky.

To. Dorset folk often say "Where do ye live to," or "bide to?" and keep other old uses of *to* as an adverb, as "Put to the hoss," "Shut to the door." So in Holstein, "An de doer war to-makt"—and the door was to maked—made to. Groth (Rothgeter): So we say "to year" for this year, as "to-day" for this day. To for at—As to whome, for at home.

TOFT. A plot of ground on which a house has stood "without toft or croft."

TOLE. To entice or allure.

TOLEBOY. A decoy.

TOOK TO. (*See* Teäke).

TOOTY. To cry in a low, broken sound.

TOP. To outdo, get over—" I'll top that."

TORRIDIDDLE. Bewildered, almost mad. "You'll dreve me torrididdle."

TOTHER. The other.

TOUSE. A slight blow with the hand. "I jist gied en a touse in the head."

TOUT (N.) Toot (S.W.) A word used mostly as the name of some hills. It meant to spy, look out, as it now means in touting by touters for customers. The touts were, I suppose, spy-hills or outlook heights in troublesome times. In Dorset are several so-called touts, as Touthill, Shaftesbury; Nettlecombe Tout; a tout by Blackmore, two touts at East, in Portland; and in Tyneham two more; Tyneham Tout and Worbarrow Tout.

TRANT meant at first a treading of the ground, or road: Tramping. In old Friesic it was used for dancing.

"Wolste en trantie mei uns ha'?"
"Wilt (thou) a dance with us have?"

TRANTER. A common carrier.

TRANTY. In Dorset means to keep to the road as a common carrier.

TRAP. A ball game.

TRAPBITTLE. A bat for the game of trap.

TRAPES. Spoken of a woman, one who tramps about boldly through thick and thin, more heedful to make way than to be spotless.

TO TRAPES. "She's always a trapesèn about."

TRENDLE. A shallow tub. Saxon trendel, a ring or round body—"An wunderlic trendel wearth ateowed abutan thare sunnan"—"A wonderful ring was seen about the sun." *Chron.* 809. "Thes monan *trendel* is ge-hál:" "The moon's orb is full." This word is sometimes wrongly spelt *trendal* in handbills—*trundle*, to roll like a circle. "Atrendlod of tham torre:" "Rolled from the high rock."—*Boethius*. In Lancashire, a *trindle* is the rim of a wheelbarrow wheel.

TRIG. To prop or hold up. "Trig the door;" or "Trig the wheel."

TRIG. Sound and firm.

TRIM. A right state. "To keep oone in trim," is to keep one in correct behaviour, or in a good state. Thence, to *trim*, a boat; to balance it, or set it in a right position. "Getrymede his folc:" "Disposed his folk." *Orosius*, iv. 10.

TRIM. To *Trim* a hedge, to cut it into good shape or state. To *shear* a hedge is to shear off any ungainly or harmsome outgrowth without any main aim of trimness in the hedge. I one day asked a man who had begun to cut a hedge whether he was going to *trim* it, and he answered "No; only to *shear* 'en.'"

TRIMMEN (an intensitive.) Great of its kind. "A trimmen crop o' grass." "A trimmen girt heâre."

TRIMMER. A great or fine thing of its kind. "That's a trimmer!" "What now, trimmer?" "What now, my fine fellow?"

TRIP. A culvert over a ditch or small watercourse. Also a fare (troop) of young pigs, or a set of goslings.

TROT. Foolish talk. "Don't hearken to her trot."

TRUCKLE. To trundle.

TRUMS or DRUMS (N.) Thrums. Twisted threads or ivy stems round a tree.

TUCK. "To tuck a rick" is to draw out the loose hay from its side in tipping it.

TUCK OUT. To eat immoderately.

TUEN. A tune.

TUG-IRON, of shafts. An iron on the shafts to hitch the traces to. Same as draïl. (*See* waggon).

TUGS. The short handles fastened on the scythe snead; called also nibs.

TUMP, *Welsh*. Twmp. A hump or tuft; a very small hillock or mound.

TUN. The chimney-top up from the ridge of the house.

TUNNIGER. A funnel for tunning liquor.

TUP. A young ram.

TURK. "A turk of a thing" is an intensitive expression, meaning a big or formidable one of its kind. "There's a turk of a rat."

TURMIT. A turnip.

TURN auver in oon's mind. To weight; to deliberate upon.

TURN. The spinning wheel with its belongings for the spinning of wool formerly to be seen in most cottages in Blackmore.

Many of the craftwords of spinning and weaving that were formerly daily on Blackmore people's lips would now be hardly understood by their after kin, such as cards, rollers, turns, spools, perns, yarn, and others. The wool spinning turn stood on a four-legged tressel, and the wheel at the near end of it was from two to three feet athwart. The spinner holding a roller of wool let it be drawn off round the running spool. If the yarn was going up to the spool too small she stepped up to it to give it more wool; if it was too thick she stepped back to give it less, so that she was often in a kind of dance not unhealthy or ungraceful, and as the wheel might be left at will for house work, she, as a wife, was a good housekeeper, or, as a girl, was daily learning to become one. The factory is or it may be a good thing for the making of capital, but it is not an excellent thing for the making of healthy and skilled housewives for poor men.

TUSSLE. A struggle or contest with another.

TUSSOCK. A grass tuft.

TUT. To do work by the tut is by the piece, or lump; not by the day.

TUTTY. A nosegay, a bunch of flowers. "And primula she takes the tutty there."—*Curtard's Caltha Poetarum*, 1599.

TWIDDICK. A small twig.

TWILADE. To load a waggon lightly and hale out, as from a coppice or bad road, and then to go back and partly load again; and lastly, hale out and take up what was unloaded.

TWIN. A twain; a two. Rightly Dorset speech says "John and Joe be a twin," not twins (twains), which must be at least four. Rent in twain, Mark xv. 38.

TWINK (W). A chaffinch.

TWIRIPE (W). Partly ripe.

TWITE. To reproach; to twit.

TWOAD, TOAD. A poor twoad is a wording of pity for one naked or helpless. A mother said of her boy who in wet weather came home every day very wet "I can hardly keep a dry rag on his back, poor twoad."

TYEN. (*See* Stall.)

U.

UNBEKNOWN. Not known of.

UNDERCREEPEN. Underhand. Working slily against another.

UNDERGROUN' JOBBLER. The bird wheatear.

UNGAINLY. Not going or working well as a means to an end. Unhandy.

UNHEAL. Uncover. Unroof.

UNRAY. To undress.

UP, to UP. To get up in the morning. "Is Jenny up? She's uppèn."

UP-ON-END. Upright.

UPPEN-STOCK. A block or stock cut into steps from which to get on horseback.

UPSIDES WI'. Even with. Having given another tit for tat.

URGE. To retch.

USE MONEY. Interest for money. "Aunt left her zome money, an' she wer to live on the use money o't till she wer 21."

V.

VALL. To fall.

VALL IN WI'. To coincide with. *Co-in-cado* (Latin) means to fall in with.

VALL OUT. To happen. Also to quarrel, "See that ye fall not out by the way"—Gen. xiv. 24.

VALL TO. To set at work. To begin.

VALL AWAY. To lose flesh. "How he's avell away;" sometimes it is said "a-pitched away."

VALIE. Value.

VAMP. The sole of a shoe.

VAN. The winnowing sheet.

VANNER. The kestrel hawk.

VANG. To take, get, earn.

VANHOLE. Of a stone quarry (Portland) fanhole.

VARDEN. A farthing.

VEAG (Saxon) *Faegth* : Wrath. A high heat of anger.

VEARE. A farrow or litter of pigs. Also to farrow [A.S. Farw].

VEARE. A weasel.

VEÄRY'S HEART. The fossil echinus, *spatanguis coranguinum*.

VEÄRY'S HEAD. The fossil echinus, the *galerites castanea*, and some other such kinds are called veäries' heads.

Veary rings. The rings of fungi so often seen in the grass of our downs, of which folklore says that they come from the dancing of the Fairies, and that the *Swams* (our forefathers' word for the Latin fungi) were the stools on which they sat to rest, and in Devon they are called pixy stools, fairy stools, though some of our folk, not giving them the honour of their own folklore, call them "Twoad stools." Mr. Abraham Crocker, formerly a land surveyor, of Frome, in Somerset, might have been one of the first who, slighting the claims of fairies and toads, wrote, many years ago, in a magazine on the growth of the "Feary rings," and on their enriching of the soil. "The fairy stools, I believe he said, after they have seeded, rot down, and the seeds which fall outward grow up in a wider ring, while those that fall inward on the ground already spent of fungus matter, do not grow." The Devon folklore calls the haws *Pixy pears*, Fairy pears, and, as the hawthorn often grows near a fairy ring on a down, it is no wonder it was thought that the fairies could help themselves to pretty small fruit so handy. Anent fungi: A worthy yeoman told the writer that he went on his down one morning and saw a mushroom and went to it to pick it, and found a gold ring on it. The mushroom had happened to spring up in the middle of the lost ring and lifted it up as it grew.

Veät. A vat, as a cheese vat.

Veath. Much as Veag. Saxon *Faegth*, a high heat of wrath.

Vell. A fell, hide, skin, or a film, as one grown over the eye. "I can't zee vell or mark o't;" also to fell or sew down.

Ve'ss. Verse.

Vess'y. To versey. To read verses by turns.

Vetch. To vetch. To fetch. To vetch the butter. To form it by churning or pumping.

Vetch. To vetch the water. To throw water into a pump with a leaky piston, so as to seal it and make it act.

Vew. Dorset says "A good vew" as well as "A good many."

Veze. To flit or fidget about. "How she do veze about the house wi' the candle."

Villet. A fillet; a cloth put round a cheese in the vat.

Vinny, Vinnied. Mouldy with a blue mould or fungus. [A.S. *fenn*, wetness. Mouldy or mildewy from damp. "Finie hlafas." Mouldy loaves—Josh. ix. 5. "The stwones be vinny." The stones are damp from condensed steam. "Blue vinny or vinnied cheese." Blue mouldy Dorset cheese.]

VITTY. Fitty, proper. "There now you do look vitty."

VLAIL. A flail.

VLANKER. A big flake of fire.

VLEAKE. A flake. A broad, stout hurdle, such as would be used for the making of a flooring of a loft in a rough shed.

VLEAKE. A flake. A bar to be fastened down on the ground, and having holes to hold the stakes on which hurdles are wattled.

VLEARE. Flare.

VLEE. To fly or flee. "It fled past 'em." Also a fly or flea.

VLEEFLAP. A handled flap to drive the flies from meat, as on the shambles.

VLESH VLEE. A flesh fly. The blow fly—*musca vomitoria*.

VLINDERS. Fast flying pieces, as of a body smashed. "He hit the jug all to vlinders."

VLINT-STWONE. The word that sounds of the stone age, as *flean* (Saxon) was a flying thing, an arrow; and "fleanet," a flint, would mean a little arrow, or the arrow head, or arrow stone. So in old Dorset the flint was a vlint-stwone, or arrow stone. We have dropped the word stone, but flint did not mean a stone.

VLITTER MOUSE. A bat.

VLOCKS. Knobs of wool; sometimes used to stuff beds.

VODDY. Foody, nourishing.

VOG. Fog.

VO'K. Folk.

VOKKET. To go about here and there.

VOLLY. To follow.

VOLLIER. A board of a cheese wring. (*See* "Steän.")

VORE-RIGHT. Taking or going right forward without looking to presence or consequences or seemliness.

VOREFRIENDS (E). Ancestors.

VOWEL. The placenta of a cow. Also a fowl.

VOWER. Four.

VROGHOPPER. (*See* Froghopper.)

VUDDICKS. A course, fat woman.

VUR (W). To throw.

Vu'st. First.

Vuz; Vuzzen. Furze.

Vwo'th. Forth, going. "Water will have its vwo'th."

W.

Wad. A big wounden wisp of hay or straw.

Wag. To stir; go. "I can hardly wag."

Waggon. To show the Dorset names of the chief parts of a waggon, it may be well to say that its axles are exes (see exe); the bottom (bed) of the waggon consists of planks on strips (shoots), reaching from side to side through mortises in timbers (summers), lying from end to end over a bearing pillar on the hinder axle, and on the two pillars (the hanging pillar and carriage pillar) bearing on the fore-axle. The fore-axle is connected with the hinder one by a thorough pole, the fore end of which has a free motion on a pin (the main pin), which takes it with the two pillars and fore-axle, and its hinder end, reaching the hinder axle, is connected by a tail bolt with the shuttle-axle, that takes the hinder end of the summers and tail board. A parallelogram of timbers is fixed on the fore-axle to take the shafts (draughts or sharps), the hinder end of which is the sweep, and the sides of which are called guides, and on them are set the slides or felloe-pieces (hounds or bussels), which bear the pillars when the waggon locks. The sides or raves are propped by brackets, called stouters or stretchers. The sharps (shafts) have in them three pairs of staples—the dräits or steäples to draw by with a chain from the collar; the ridge tie steäples, to take the ridge tie passing over the cart-tree on the thiller's back, and keeping up the shafts; and the breechen steäple, to take the breeching.

Wags. "The birds have aplaïed the wags wi' the pease." In some parts wag is given for wags. I fear the word wags may mean very naughty beings.

Wagwanton. Quaking grass (briza).

Wanleäss. A windlass as of a cider wring.

Ware (E). A sheep walk, as Tillywhim Ware, near Swanage.

Washdish. Dishwasher, Pollywashdish, the water wagtail.

Watshed. Wetshod.

Waxen Crundels or Kernels. Enlarged tonsils, glands of the neck.

Way. A roller used in launching of the great stone boats at Swanage.

Wayzalt. A children's game in which two, locking their arms together behind, back to back, lift each other by turns from the ground.

Wease. A wreath or crown of wool put on the head to take the milk pail. (The writer has often seen a milkwoman walk on with the pail unstayed, on her head, knitting with her hands.) Wease is also a wisp of hay or straw, with which, dipped in milk, a calf is suckled.

Weäle. (*See* "Haymeäkèn.")

Weave (E). To rock backwards and forwards as in pain.

Week's end. Saturday night.

Well. A word in many names of Dorset places, as Askerswell, Holwell, and Pokeswell. Well meant at first a well-spring, and not a dug pit. Saxon, "Well-an," to roll, as water rolling out a spring, or boiling, thence it meant to boil.

Well-to-do. In easy circumstances.

Welshnut. The walnut. Welsh and wal (weäl) both mean foreign.

Welm. A water spring, a welling up of water, as Toller "Welm," the springhead of the Toller stream.

Werden. Were or was not.

Werret. To worry.

Wevvet. Wivet, a cobweb. "That cloth is so thin's a wevvet."

Wey and Bodkins. A set of spreaders for the hitching of two horses to the same part of a sull or harrow. The wey is, or was, fastened at its middle to the sull or harrow by a cops—an iron bow with a free joint, and the bodkins are, or were, fastened by a crook on their middle to *clipses* on the two ends of the wey and had the traces hitched by *clipses* to their two ends. They were sometimes called wheppenses.

Whack, Whang. A blow as from a stick in a strongly swung arm.

When. Used thus—any-when, zome-when, noo-when.

Whence "Wallop." To boil in a small way as in a pot, and "Potwalloper" a potboiler, a voter who boiled his own pot on his own fire; also

"**Wallow.**" To roll; and

"**Welter.**" To roll slightly about, and the German "waltz," a roller and a rolling dance.

Whimsay. What whirls, a whirling machine.

Whimper. To whine much and shrill.

WHINDLEN. Small and weakly, spoken of a child, or of a plant.

WHICKER. To neigh as a horse.

WHINNICK. To whine softly or slightly.

WHIPPENS. Whoppens:
"Half-a-groat want twopence:
"Blows More kicks than halfpence."

WHIPFAGGOTS. Faggots made of the tips of wood cut off at hurdlemaking.

WHIP'SWHILE. The time of smacking a whip. "Ev'ry whip'swhile I be ahindered by oone or tother."

WHIRLIGIG. A plaything, mostly made of a round and round-headed stick, hanging through holes at the top and bottom of a nutshell, with an apple on its lower end. It is whirled by a string coiled round it.

WHITTLE. A child's woollen napkin.

WHIVER. To hover, also to quiver.

WHOP. A blow from a strongly swung arm.

WHOG. Go off to the right, spoken to horses.

WHUR. To fling overhanded.

WI'. With.

WIDDICK. A small withy or rod.

WILLY-BASKET. A large withy-basket.

WILLY-NILLY. Willing or not willing. [A.S. Willig nillig for ne willig.]

WIND MOW. A small mow of sheaves made for a time in the field.

WINK. A winch or crank.

WITHWIND. Withywind. The Bindweed.

WITHY-HANGER. The bird "Tree creeper."

WIZZEN. The windpipe

WOBLET. The handle of a hayknife.

WONT. Want, a mole. There is a Dorset pun on the word wont, or want, a mole. "Why do Mr. N. zell his land?" Answer—"Because the wonts (wants) be in it."

WONT-HILL. A mole-hill.

WOODCULVER, Woodcu'ver (E). L being dropped a bad form of the word. Culfer called also the "Woodquest" or "Quist." The woodpigeon or ringdove. Columbus, Palumbus, Scotch; "Arshatt" from the S., "cusc," chaste, and "cusceote," called quest, quist, or quice, from a word root meaning to complain, whine.

WOODWEX, Woadwaxen. *Genista Tinctoria.* Dyers' greenweed.

WOOLCOMBER. The trade of woolcomber is often found in the old jury lists of Blackmore men. The wool was combed, or carded, by two cards (keärds) with square backs like brush backs and with handles, but faced with wire instead of bristles, and the wool was pulled for a while between the cards, and then rolled off in rollers. The "o" in roller has the sound of "o" in collar. A tale (*valeat quantum*) was formerly told of an idle wife in Blackmore, who took in wool to card, and after too long a time had carded only two or three rollers; and began to fear a scolding from her husband, who knew not as yet the truth of the wool, but believed in the witchcraft of Gammer, A.B. In the night she aroused her man with "O, I've ahad twice the seäme dreäm that A.B. had bewitched all my rollers back again into loose wool. I'm sure it must true. Do now step down an' zee." John did so, and came back with "'Tis true enough. The rollers be out again in loose wool all but two or dree, an' they be so slack that they'll soon volly the rest."

WO'OSE. Worse.

WOPS. A wasp. Waeps, with ps for sp, is the old Saxon form of the word, and our brethren of Holstein still call a wasp *en weps*.

WORDLE. World.

WORM. A small tool for winding or twisting of hay bands.

WORNAIL, Wornil. The larva of the cowfly *Tabanus (oestrus bovis)*, growing under the skin of the back of cattle.

WORRET. To worry in small matters, teaze.

WOTSHED (N), Wetshod, Wetshoed. "For weetshoed thei gone." *Piers Plowman.*

WRACK. "Mind, you'll stan' the wrack o't;" "You will stand the consequences."

WRAG. To scold; to accuse with bitter words. "Of thèm the ge hine wrègath."—Luke xxiii. 14.

WRANCH. A tool, a spanner, as a screw-wranch for the turning of square-headed screws in machines.

WRIDE. A bush of many stems from one root; as, a wride of hazel or ash; or the family of stalks growing from one grain. "Thurh thòne lea to thàm miclam hæsl wride;" "Through the field to the great hazel wride (bush)."—A Charter of Eàdmund, A.D. 944.

WRIDE. To wride out; to throw out stalks. "The wheat do wride out well."

WRIG. Part of the cider harness "cider from the wrig," ere put into a cask.

WRIGGLES. Plates of a fossil pentacrinite found about Batcombe, of which it was found that if they are spread in vinegar on the bottom of a plate, they will go wrigglingly, and cluster up in the middle of the plate. *Probatum est* with vinegar. The writer never tried them in water.

WRING. A press; as a cider-wring. "And sette thæaon win wringan." Matt. xxi. 33. In a tract of the "Library of Useful Knowledge" on Geology, there is given a wood-cut of a pile of rock called a *cheese-wring*, which is wrongly spelt *cheese-ring*.

WRITH. The bond of a faggot. A little wreath of a twisted wand to hold a hurdle to the sowel.

WRIX. To wreathe or writh up, to wattle up, as to wrix a gap in a hedge, with wrix, rods, or furze.

WROUT. To grub up, as pigs do the ground.

WULL. Will.

WUST. Wouldest. Wouldest thou.

WUT. Woot. Wilt thou? "Lend me thy knife, woot?"

Y.

YANDER (N.) Yonder.

YEAN (N). To lamb; spoken of a ewe. S. *Yeaenian*.

YEAT-SMASHER (E). "The bird wheatear."

YEOTEN. Veät.

YEOTEN STWONE. Yoting vat.

YOP. Yelp.

YOTING STONE. A stonen cistern formerly used in Dorset, as elsewhere, in brewing. Its use was that of the mashing-vat. Some time ago it was asked among some antiquarians what was a yoting stone, and some working man said he thought it was a trough for pigs' food. In the old court books of Frampton Court, kindly put under my hand by Mr. Sheridan, I find in some inventories given in on the proving of wills, and the yoating vat was among brewing utensils. In 1678 we find "two yoating vauts;" in 1679, "the yoating howse"—the mashing house; but in 1682 and 1709 the name "yoating vat" gives place to "meashing vate or vat." Dr. Prior, author of "The Popular Names of British Plants, &c.," very kindly sent me some quotations from a book by Gervasse Markham, 1631, who, in speaking on brewing, says that of the two kinds of "vats or cesternes coopers' worke (fatts) of wood, and masons' worke (cesternes made of stone), the cesterne of stone is much the better," and tells wherefore. The yoting stone was so called from the Saxon *geótan*. To pour out, and was the mashing vat. "Ic teárâs sceal *geótan*." I shall shed tears. *Cynewulf*.

YOICKS. A cry of following in a chase.

YOLLER. Yollow, yellow.

YOLLOW WOPS (N). Yellow wasp not the hornet.

Z.

ZA, ZAW. To saw.

ZACK. A sack, zand.

ZEALE. A sale.

ZEAM. A seam.

ZEBM. Seven.

ZEDGE. Sedge.

ZEDGEMOCK. A tuft or bunch of sedge grass.

ZEE'D. Saw. I zee'd you.

ZEED. Seed.

ZEEDLIP. A seed box in which a sower (broadcast) carries his seed.

ZENNIT. Seven-night, a week. "This day ze'nni't." This day week, so this day *vort-night—fourteen-night*. A week is in Welsh *wythnos*. *Eight-night*, and we, indeed, take in the wholes or halves of eight nights as we take the last half of one Sunday night and the first half of the next. Some scholars have wondered why some races, as ours and the Celtic, reckoned by nights rather than by days. Well, they reckoned months by the moon, and took the quarters of the moon for weeks, as we call them. With the Britons the times for the holding of the lower common meetings (Gorseddau) for civil and religious business were new and full moons, and its first and third quarters: once a week, and since the moon measured the times and was to be seen by night and not by day, they reckoned by nights, and from mid-night to mid-night as we do, and so reckoned in wholes or halves their *wythnos*—eight-night.

ZET. Set, as zet down.

ZET OFF, zet out. To start.

ZET TO.

ZET UP. To make angry. "He wer zoo zet up a bout it."

ZEW. Sew.

ZEW. Azew, which see.

ZICH. Such.

ZIDE. Side.

ZIDELAND. Slanting, sloping.

ZIFT. Sift.

ZILLGREEN. Houseleek.

ZILT. A vessel to salt meat in. [A.S. Syltan, to salt. A vessel for salting meat in. "Ælc man bith mid fyre gesylt"—Mark ix. 49. As a silt is so called from Syltan to salt.]

ZINK. Sink.

ZIT. Sit.

ZIVE. A scythe. Whence came the form scythe, and above all the c in it? I cannot tell, as there is not any such form in sister tongues—German, Dutch, Friesic, or Icelandic.

ZIVES. Chives.

ZOCK. A sock.

ZOG. Sog, soak, sink.

ZOGGY. Sinky, soaky; as wet soft ground.

ZOGGY. Soggy, heavy to lift. "You be a zoggy young chap," spoken to a heavy child. Now this word *soggy* for wet, loose ground, and a *soggy*, or heavy, child, seems at first thought to be, as it is not, two sundry words of most unlike meanings. Such cases are interesting and useful in speech-lore, as leading to the first meaning of word-roots. These uses of "soggy" help to show that the first broad meaning of the root, and even the root head *s*, was that of sinkingness. "'Soggy' ground" is sinky ground, into which the foot will *sink* as water has *sunk* into it, and "soggy" (heavy) child is a *sinky* child with a strong sinking force or weight with which the heaving upholding force must be even or it would sink and fall, and that heaving force is called in Dorset *heft*, which means the force that will match, or in lifting will overcome, the sinking force or sogginess.

ZOME. Some.

ZOMEHAT. Somewhat, something.

ZOOT. Soot.

ZOP. Sop.

ZORRY. Sorry.

ZOT. Sat. Past time of sit.

ZOUNDY, Soune (O). To swoon. Saxon swindan, "Medland swound. The King sowned and Sir Lucan fyl in a sowne." Sir Thomas Malory, Capitulum V., by Skeat. "For so daine sorrow swounded down" (*Ovid's Metamorphosis*).

ZOWEL. A sowel, which see.

ZULL. Saxon sulh, syl, a plough. "Nán-man the his hand a-set on his sulh." No man who hath set his hand on his plough—Saxon, Luke ix. 62.

ZULL PADDLE. A paddle to cleazen the hanfurrow of clingy dirt.

ZUMMERLEAZE. A leaze, unmown ground for summer feed.

ZUMMERMWOLDS. Summermoulds, freckles on the face.

ZUMMERS OF A WAGGON. (*See* Waggon.)

ZUN. Sun.

ZUN. Back-zunned. Said of a house having a northern aspect, and its back to the sun.

ZWAIL. To sway about from side to side. To swagger.

ZWATH. The ridge of grass of the track of one mower, or his track itself. "Nyle he ænig swæthe æfre forlætan." "Nor will he ever forsake any track."

ZWEAL. To singe; to scorch; to burn the outside. "See sunne hit forswælde." "The sun scorched it up."—Mark iv. 6. "Do ye scald your pigs, ar zweal em?" "He is lik' a swealed cat; better than 'e do look var." [A.S. Swelan.]

I gladly thank many friends and well wishers for the words they have so kindly sent me in answer to my request in the *Dorset County Chronicle*:— Rev. C. R. Baskett, chaplain to the Bishop of New Westminster, Chillewach; the late Canon Bingham; Rev. N. Bond, Tyneham; Rev. O. P. Cambridge, Bloxworth; Mr. James Cross, Wimborne; Mr. J. Albert Drew, Wareham; Mr. G. W. Floyer, Stafford; Mr. W. P. Fletcher, Wimborne; Mr. James Forrester, Brianston; Rev. C. E. W. Fox, Askerswell.—Mr. Thomas Hardy, Dorchester; Rev. Walter Kendall, East Lulworth, an interesting collection of carefully gathered and marked words and forms of words of East Dorset; Mr. J. V. Lawrance, Weymouth, some Dorset verses written by a prisoner of Dorchester Gaol; Mr. H. J. Moule, Dorchester; Mr. L. Lionel Parsons, Stalbridge; Miss Price, Mary-street, Swanage; Rev. Spencer Smith, Kingston, Wareham; Mr. H. W. Truman, for an earlier contribution; Rev. J. L. Warner, Tarrant Gunville; Mrs. Barrett

INDEX TO THE GRAMMAR.

	PAGE.
a, for e	4
a, as in "abound," past participle	27
ae, for aw	4
aÿ for ay	4
Breath pennings	6
bm for vn	14
Dorset expressions	35
d for th	9
d out	13
Do, help g verb	39
eä, for ea	2
ea, for a	3
ê, for ea	2
em, for them	2
en, for him	17
en, plural ending	17
en, adjective ending	17
es, plural	36
He, for it	39
I, for me	39
ks for sk	11
Nominative, for objective case-form	39
Number	16 and 36
Numerals	20
oo, for o	5
ou, for u	5
Pronouns	20
Pronouns, A.S. and Dorset	37
ps, for sp	12
r, aspirate	9
r out before s	10
r out, self	20
Theäse and thik	17
They, for those	38
u for i	2
Verbs	21
Weak and strong verbs	41
wei for oi	4
wo for o	4
y verb, end g	23
v, for f	8

CPSIA information can be obtained at www.ICGtesting.com
Printed in the USA
BVOW06s1800201213

339719BV00010B/456/P